BECOMING FRIENDS, PARTNERS, & LOVERS

THE GUIDEBOOK

KEVIN A. THOMPSON
WITH RANDY NORDELL

BECOMING
FRIENDS, PARTNERS &LOVERS

THE GUIDEBOOK

KEVIN A. THOMPSON
WITH RANDY NORDELL

THRIVE
MEDIA

CONTENTS

Introduction   7

SESSION 1   Begin with Intention   11

SESSION 2   Friendship and Trust   15

SESSION 3   Understanding Yourself and Your Spouse   23

SESSION 4   Having Fun and Rest   31

SESSION 5   Partnership and Respect   41

SESSION 6   Money   49

SESSION 7   Work   57

SESSION 8   Communication and Conflict   67

SESSION 9   Others   77

SESSION 10   Prioritize Sex   87

SESSION 11   Intimacy and Vulnerability   95

SESSION 12   Faith   107

Bibliography   116

Author Bios   117

INTRODUCTION

When I wrote *Friends, Partners & Lovers,* I focused on one question: what should a spouse do? As we are about to see, that book lays out the three basic roles of a spouse. It gives a basic overview of marriage as designed in Genesis 2.

This guidebook builds on that original idea but has a unique purpose. It's meant to be processed not by an individual or even a couple but as a group. Whether it be a small group study or a marriage mentoring relationship, sharing our journey with others creates challenge, support, and encouragement to pursue God's best.

HOW TO USE THE GUIDEBOOK

This is a guidebook. It intends to spark ideas and create conversation—individually, with you as a couple, and with others. While the content is important, it's not the only thing. Transformation takes place at the intersection of good content and healthy community. Don't ignore the content. Yet also don't elevate it above the meaningful relationships that can be formed in a group study.

We often associate with other couples with whom we have things in common: a similar outlook on life, our schedules, and our mutual interests. For the purpose of this study, those things may or may not be present. More important than common interests is a common purpose—experiencing the fullness of what marriage can be. Healthy community isn't characterized by everyone being alike. It's defined as a group of people devoted to supporting one another in the pursuit of a better marriage.

Notice: whether you are leading a group, mentoring another couple, being mentored or attending a study, your job with others is NOT to be their counselor. That's not the role they need. You don't tell them what to do. You don't solve their problems. You don't freely give your opinions about what they are facing. While there may be times to share things that have worked within your own life and marriage, mostly you are there for support. Encourage them to explore, be vulnerable, consider the content, and find new patterns of behavior which might lead to better relational health. If a couple has unique difficulties, you might encourage them toward clinical counseling, but you will never attempt to play that role.

The guidebook is divided into twelve sessions. The first session is intentionally brief so you can share your story. The rest of the sessions have teaching, questions for personal reflection, things to discuss as a couple, and group discussion questions. All the questions are simply there to inspire thought and conversation.

Each person should have their own book. Why? Because every person should be equally committed and invested in the process. When each couple only gets one book, one spouse becomes responsible. This quickly devolves into one spouse doing the reading, one spouse doing the work, and only one spouse helping move the marriage forward. Instead, we want full investment from both spouses. Both should bring their workbook, answer the questions, and take the initiative in helping the relationship grow.

RESOURCES AND THE ASSESSMENT

At changetheodds.com is a simple assessment each couple should take at the beginning and end of marriage mentoring. The assessment serves as a baseline to help the couples discover some areas of strength and other potential areas of improvement. While the overall score matters, individual questions are more critical. Consider why each question matters and how progress in that area can assist the overall satisfaction of your relationship. Regularly review the questions and focus on adapting the actions and attitudes behind the questions into your daily routine.

Also on the website are further resources to assist the process. Videos, podcasts, articles, and books can help you dive deeper into each session.

Go to **changetheodds.com/becomingfpl** for more. Or, scan the QR code:

THE PERSPECTIVE

This book is a companion to *Friends, Partners & Lovers: What it takes to make your marriage work*. The lessons and assessments are built around these three specific roles that each spouse should play in the life of the one they love. All three are equally important and impact one another. Improvement in one area will likely lead to progress in the other two. Struggle in one area will flow into other areas.

WHY FRIENDS, PARTNERS & LOVERS?

"What makes marriage work is predictable, universal, and completely under our control" pg. 28 Friends, Partners & Lovers (FPL).

Imagine starting a new job, and your boss never gives you a job description. Expectations are present. Your co-workers assume what you should do and how that impacts their work. Those outside the business will interact with you, believing you have a specific role. Everyone thinks they know what you should be doing, but this may be the first time anyone has told you your specific role. What do you do? It would be easy to figure out when you should arrive and when to leave work. After paying attention to your co-workers for a few days, that would be understood. But you still wouldn't know what to do. You could do what you think is right or what others believe you should do, but what is most needed is for your boss to write a clear job description, assign tasks and responsibilities, and clarify boundaries.

Most people walk into marriage without a clear job description. They guess, do what their parents did, or do whatever comes naturally, but those actions are rarely the totality of what their spouse needs or what a good marriage demands.

Thankfully, there is a job description. The designer of marriage also described the three basic roles of a good husband or wife. When we say, "I do," these are the three things we are agreeing to do.

Friend. At the foundation of any good marriage is deep friendship. By no means should a spouse be your only friend, but they should be your best friend. Throughout a marriage, spouses will spend a tremendous amount of time together and should enjoy being in the presence of one another. Deep levels of trust, admiration, and respect should define every marriage.

Many marriages struggle because they begin as a friendship, but they do not continue to develop the friendship through the marriage. They assume it will happen naturally, but no friendship naturally sustains itself. It takes intention and effort. Others make a grand mistake when they do not see friendship as an essential aspect of whom to marry. Saying you wouldn't want to ruin the friendship is ignorance of the true nature of marriage. Marry a friend and then work your whole life to build the friendship.

Partner. Marriage is a business decision. Many people live in denial of this reality, but it is true. Those who doubt the business side of marriage get a rude awakening if the marriage fails and ends up in divorce court. In the past, marriage was often seen as nothing more than a business decision. Kings expanded their territory, made alliances, and played political games through marriage.

Marriage should never be only a business decision, but business must be seen as a component. While some couples work closely together and others completely separate work from home life, no one should foolishly ignore that every spouse is a business partner—they influence your credit score, determine how you spend money, and own half of everything you own. One should never marry for business, but one should always keep business in mind. A good spouse is also a good business partner. They may not know all the business details, but they know you well enough to point out blind spots and encourage strengths.

Lover. The significant difference between friendship and marriage is the element of sexuality. While every marriage should include friendship, only one friendship should consist of sexual intimacy. That is marriage. This aspect of marriage should neither be elevated as the most essential part of marriage nor should it be diminished into a secondary role within the marital relationship. Sex is not the only thing, but it is an important thing for the marital covenant. While most relationships start strong in sexuality—it's often a driving factor for marriage—many couples falsely assume this aspect of marriage should develop naturally with little effort. It's a dangerous assumption. A strong sexual connection takes time, knowledge, wisdom, understanding, and a lot of trial and error.

These three roles are integrally woven together. When one is lacking, it greatly impacts the other two. When one is improved, it has a ripple effect in the other areas. The simplest way to view it is like a three-legged stool. When one leg is a little short, the stool can stand, but it has a bit of a wobble. However, when a leg or two is greatly diminished from another leg, the stool can neither hold weight nor stand.

Tragically, far too many relationships are lacking in one of the three main areas. When intimacy is missing from a strong friendship and partnership, the couple devolves into a roommate-type relationship. They live parallel lives, supporting each other in making the household operate but lacking the unique connection intended for marriage. When partnership is missing, a couple reverts to a boyfriend/girlfriend relationship with benefits. They lack the maturity that a strong marriage offers. And when friendship is missing, the marriage becomes more like a business arrangement.

Marriage can be so much more than many people experience. A friend is someone always by your side. A partner is someone who always has your back. A lover is someone who sees you and loves you in the fullness of who you are. Imagine always having someone by your side who has your back and loves you fully. That's the design of marriage. Your job description as a spouse is to be those three things to your husband or wife.

SESSION 1

BEGIN WITH INTENTION

"Marriage isn't the flip of a coin; it's the flip of the will." (pg. 19, FPL)

INTENTION BROUGHT YOU HERE

Chances are, you're not here by accident. You took the brave (and scary) step of looking at each other and realizing your marriage may not be exactly what you intended it to be when you were dating or early in your married life. ***You intentionally chose to be here…congrats!***

- Mentees: Share your story with your mentors. Include details about your family life growing up, your dating life, your married life, and where you are now.
- Mentors: Share your marriage journey. Describe some of the challenges and the areas of growth along the way.

MORE ABOUT INTENTION

Have you ever seen an old friend after many years and noticed they are in tremendous shape? When you ask the person how they experienced such a great achievement, they will never say: "It was the strangest thing. I went into a grocery store and suddenly found myself in the produce section, so I just began to buy produce, and from that day forward I ate healthy" or "I was driving down the road, and my car veered into the parking lot of a workout facility, so I went inside and started working out."

People do not lose weight by accident. They don't get into shape by coincidence. It happens with a conscious decision. And not just one decision. It's a continual series of decisions until new habits are formed. Even then, they must <u>intentionally practice new habits</u> to ensure they do not slide into old behaviors.

- As it is with weight loss, exercise, or any meaningful change, *every positive change begins with intention.*
- *We never drift into something good,* so don't let your relationship be left to fate.
- *A healthy marriage is available to every couple.*
- *Lasting love doesn't just happen.* It's built, created, and sustained.
- The key to building such a love is *intention.*

Because *intention* is the key to a healthy marriage, *apathy should be viewed as our greatest threat.* In most cases, divorce is not the byproduct of bad intentions. It's the result of no intention. People don't run into affairs; they drift into them. They don't race toward living parallel lives; they gradually grow apart. Apathy can come from a variety of sources:

Fear: Effort implies passion. To engage in one's relationship with intention is to make oneself vulnerable. The spouse who appears to care the least has the most control. To show intention is to <u>have the courage to let go of power.</u>

- We may not show intention in our relationship because *we're afraid of what might happen.*
- Fear of vulnerability, rejection, being wrong, and change make apathy more appealing than intention.
- *Apathy driven by fear does not make life easier.* It makes it more difficult.
- *Intention* is always worth the effort.

Believing in a soul mate: We have long been told that there is a perfect soul mate who completes us. If that person exists, there is no need to put energy into our relationships. We should find the right person, and then the rest of the marriage will be easy. But, of course, no person is perfect, and a soul mate doesn't exist.

- Creating and building love demands ongoing effort.
- We don't discover a soul mate.
- "Sole" mates become "soul" mates through decades of effort.

Flip of a coin: Most people believe that a good marriage is just the flip of a coin. Whether they work hard or not doesn't matter. If we believe our effort does not matter, we are far less likely to do the work.

- Our intention dramatically changes the odds of marriage.
- Understanding the value of our efforts greatly increases the likelihood that we will continue to be intentional.
- The chance of success of a marriage is not 50/50.
- By doing the work, a couple can greatly increase the odds of a successful marriage.

Most people believe that a failed marriage is the byproduct of adultery, financial struggles, an inability to communicate, or a conscious choice to live a different life. It's not. In most cases, those potentially fatal circumstances in a marriage are symptoms of a greater disease…apathy. While the perception of many is that a bad marriage is full of anger, far more often, it's not. Most marriages that die do so with a whimper, not a shout. The antidote is intention…intentional communication, sex, connection, faith, money management, time together, effort, and more effort. Work that's worth it.

———————

Because *intention* is the key to a healthy marriage, *apathy should be viewed as our greatest threat.*

———————

DISCUSS IT AS A GROUP

When thinking about a couple you'd describe as happy, what intentional actions do you see them consistently make?

Of the three sources of apathy listed (fear, soul mate, flip of a coin), which are you most likely to feel/believe? Why do you think this is so?

Identify an area in your relationship where you have been apathetic. What specifically can you do this week to change that?

FRIENDS, PARTNERS & LOVERS - THE GUIDEBOOK

What are four intentional steps you can take to improve your relationship?

PRACTICE IT - BE INTENTIONAL

With your spouse, set aside a specific time this week to discuss the state of your relationship. Talk about your expectations for marriage mentoring over these next six months or so.

Make a list of questions to ask your mentors the next time you get together.

Much of what you get out of this study depends upon your intentionality. Plan with your spouse how you will be intentional about preparing for meetings with your mentors.

- When will you review the session material and answer the questions in the **Think About It** section?

- When will you take time with your spouse to discuss the questions in the **Talk About It** section?

Most marriages die with a whimper, not a shout. *The antidote is intention.*

DIGGING DEEPER

Friends, Partners, and Lovers by Kevin A. Thompson. Chapter 1 "The Number One Cause of Divorce."

The Good News About Marriage by Shaunti Feldhahn. This book addresses the myth that 50% of marriages end in divorce.

"The Importance of Intentionality in Our Relationships."
Better Together Family Therapy. https://betterfamilytherapy.com/blog/intentional-relationships

"10 Tips on How to Set Intentional in a Relationship." By Rachael Pace.
Marriage.com: https://www.marriage.com/advice/relationship/intention-in-relationship/

SESSION 2

"Friendship is built on shared attention." (pg. 42, FPL)

Friendship is built side by side. My earliest friendships were formed in the classroom with those sitting next to me. Together, we experienced (and endured) life as it came at us. The shared experience is what helped create these lasting relationships.

A wedding ceremony often begins and ends with the couple standing side-by-side, listening to the minister. In the middle, they face each other to repeat vows, but they stand together shoulder to shoulder for most of the service. This is a great image of what a strong friendship entails. Our bond is created as we experience life together as equals, side by side.

Trust is everything. Without it, genuine friendships and relationships cannot exist. With it, there is no limit to what a connection can achieve. It's the foundation of marriage because it is the key ingredient to a healthy friendship.

The first realization regarding trust must be an understanding that trust is never given; it is always earned. Imagine how foolish it would be to walk up to someone in Wal-Mart and say, "I'm going to trust you forever." Obviously, we would never do that. Trust is a quality that a person earns over time. While we can assume the best in someone and give them an initial opportunity, what they do with that determines our level of trust.

MORE ABOUT FRIENDSHIP AND TRUST

Not all of life can be experienced side-by-side. There are places where one spouse leads the other. There are times in which we live separate lives. While we can't live every moment side-by-side, when we fail to live any moment that way, we are hindering a healthy marriage. Here are four elements of a healthy *friendship:*

Time

- *Friendship requires time.* As life gets busy, it's easy for a husband and wife to spend less and less time together.
- Between work, kids, and life, *many areas demand our time.* A smart couple will *intentionally* find time to spend together.
- Quality time is important, but *one aspect of quality time is the quantity of time.* Happy couples prioritize time with one another as they experience life side-by-side.

Shared Attention

- A key element of connection is *sharing attention.*
- A couple must *intentionally turn toward one another.*
- Each spouse needs to *bring good into the relationship*—good stories, good ideas, and things that bring warmth to life.
- *Connection is built* when each spouse focuses on the other. But when they fail to share attention, their relationship is strained.

Communication

- *Communication is vital to friendship.* A husband and wife must be in continual communication. Without it, friendship cannot exist.
- Good friends can often *communicate with just a look.*
- The longer a relationship continues, the more likely it is that they *begin to assume rather than talk.* They may think they already know what the other believes or thinks.
- A silent marriage is more of a threat than one with lots of shouting. Yet neither is desired.
- A healthy relationship is characterized by *continual communication.*

Feelings

- A key element of friendship is a *revelation of our hearts.*

- Many of us *struggle to identify and communicate our feelings.* Instead, we often deny and ignore our feelings.
- In a healthy marriage, husband and wife l*earn how to bring their feelings to the surface and share those with one another.*
- A healthy marriage and friendship *create a safe environment* to communicate feelings with one another openly.

TRUST CAN BE BROKEN

Friendship is built on *trust.* Knowing trust is built brings the reality that trust can be broken. It's fragile. No matter how long it has developed, we are not sure it will be present tomorrow. We must continually cultivate trust while also being aware that at any moment, a single act of foolishness can undo the good work we have done. Trust is primarily broken in one of two ways:

Explosion

- One dramatic failure—things like an affair, financial deceit, a foolish choice, or addiction —can destroy the trust that took decades to build.
- When an explosion happens, a couple immediately knows trust is broken, which provides the opportunity for them to recognize it and get to work on rebuilding it.

Erosion

- *Trust can be destroyed by the slow drip of inconsistency.* Failing to do what you say, apathy, selfishness, dishonor, an unwillingness to protect the spouse's heart, or a general failure to love can slowly erode trust.
- *The difficulty of erosion is that it often happens without awareness.* We don't realize trust has been lost until we wake up one day and notice we don't fully believe our spouse is for us.

TRUST CAN BE REBUILT

While the breaking of trust is tragic, the situation is not hopeless.   Trust can be rebuilt. The loss of trust does also not ensure the failure of the relationship. However, an inability to rebuild trust does guarantee a continually dysfunctional marriage. When a couple does the work, they can rebuild trust. Here are a few steps to rebuilding trust:

Acknowledge It Has Been Broken

- *Trust begins with truth.* Until we recognize that trust has been broken, it cannot be rebuilt.
- *Acknowledgment requires ownership.* If one party has broken the trust, they must take responsibility for their actions. If both parties are responsible, then both spouses must recognize their role.
- *Rebuilding trust is a two-person process.* Both husband and wife must play an active part in rebuilding trust.

Define The Goal

- A couple should state that *they desire to rebuild what has been lost.* This must be a goal to which both are committed.
- By stating the goal, both parties are *more likely to prioritize the process.*
- If a husband or wife is not willing to say they desire to build (rebuild) trust, that is a major red flag within the relationship.

Small Actions Over Time

- *Consistency + Time = Trust.*
- Trust can only be rebuilt slowly, brick by brick, action by action.
- *Rebuilt trust never happens as quickly as we desire;* time is a necessary ingredient.

Don't Overlook Failure

- *Building trust doesn't mean perfection.*
- Trust is most often built in *how we handle our mistakes:* recognize our wrong actions, admit them, seek forgiveness, and learn from our mistakes.

There is no way to overestimate the *importance of trust in a relationship.* It is so vital that a couple should prioritize building trust. In the end, trust is simple. When trust is present, I can confidently say my spouse loves me and is for me. This becomes the lens through which everything is experienced. When two people are confident the other loves them and is for them, there is no limit to what they can accomplish.

THINK ABOUT IT BY YOURSELF

Think about when you and your spouse were dating. What were some of the activities you enjoyed doing together?
Do you still do some of these activities together? Are there other activities you now enjoy doing together as friends? If not, why not?

As a couple, what is your biggest communication struggle? In what ways can strengthening your friendship improve that weakness?

Describe someone you trust. How does the presence of trust positively impact every aspect of the relationship?

Do you trust your spouse? Do you believe your spouse trusts you?

What are the things your spouse does that build your trust in them? What are the things your spouse does that erode your trust in them?

TALK ABOUT IT AS A COUPLE

Take turns sharing with your spouse some of your favorite memories from when you were dating and early married.

Ask yourselves, in what ways do we regularly and intentionally schedule time together for activities we enjoy doing together?

Discuss with your spouse some of the things that you and your spouse focus on together. How do you share attention?

Share specific things your spouse does to build trust in them.

What are actions that erode your trust in one another?

Describe to your spouse a time in which you felt your spouse was clearly beside/for you.

Between work, kids, and life, *many areas demand our time*. A smart couple will *intentionally* find time to spend together.

DISCUSS IT AS A GROUP

What was your friendship score on the assessment?

What have been some of your favorite moments during your dating and marriage years? Do you still have common activities and interests you do together?

Are you spending adequate time together for your friendship to develop? What are some of the barriers to spending quality and quantity time together? How can you navigate some of these barriers?

What makes you feel most supported by your spouse during both ordinary and challenging times in life?

Are there specific things you've done to negatively affect trust in your relationship?

What do you intentionally do to build trust in your marriage?

There is no way to overestimate the ***importance of trust in a relationship***. It is so vital that a couple should prioritize building trust as their top priority.

PRACTICE IT - BE INTENTIONAL

Intentionally plan an activity you can do together as friends at least once a week for the next two weeks.

One night this week and next week, spend time before going to bed talking about memories from your dating and early marriage years. Also, talk about shared interests and goals over the next year and the following year.
Schedule time together to have an honest discussion about trust in your marriage. Talk about ways your spouse has built trust. Also, truthfully and thoughtfully describe how you have contributed to a lack of trust.

DIGGING DEEPER

Friends, Partners, and Lovers by Kevin A. Thompson. Chapter 3, "No Wonder You Don't Love Each Other," and Chapter 4, "The Most Overlooked Characteristic of Marriage."

SESSION 3

UNDERSTANDING YOURSELF AND YOUR SPOUSE

"Deep levels of trust, admiration, and respect should define every marriage." (pg. 33, FPL)

As we get to know our partner while dating, we welcome and love their quirky qualities. We are drawn to this person precisely because he or she is different from us. This infatuation and curiosity about their personality, opinions, and preferences continues throughout the dating phase and typically carries on into the engagement, honeymoon, and first few months of marriage. However, what initially attracts us eventually frustrates us. Many of these "cute" differences eventually become not-so-cute and maybe even annoying. Additionally, before marriage, we tend to be on our best behavior and guard or even hide some aspects of our personality and preferences from our partner.

Marriage joins two unique, imperfect, and broken people together in close proximity. The better we understand one another's unique personalities and preferences, the easier it is to appreciate and celebrate the differences in our partners. God uses our personality differences in marriage to chip off some of our rough edges and improve each other.

In this session, we will look at personality styles and love languages. Many personality inventories exist, such as Meyers & Briggs, DISC, The Big Five, and Enneagram. Also, much has been written about love languages, love styles, attachment styles, and spiritual pathways. This session will not examine all the different personality inventories but rather look at the Enneagram for personality styles and the love languages introduced by Gary Chapman in his book, *The Five Love Languages.*

MORE ABOUT PERSONALITY STYLES AND LOVE LANGUAGES

Limitations of Personality Assessments and Love Language
While personality inventories and love languages are extremely useful for understanding ourselves and our spouses better, they have some limitations.

- **Categories:** While personality and love language assessments have distinct categories, most of us don't fall exactly into one category.
- **Change:** As we grow, mature, and experience life, we change, and our personality styles and love languages may also change over time.
- **Excuses:** We should not use our personality type or love language preference to excuse bad behavior.
- **Judging:** We should not judge others negatively because they have a different personality style or love language.
- **Preferences:** Personality style is different from preferences. Many of our preferences—food, activities, cleanliness, religious beliefs, politics, communication, conflict styles, etc.—originate from our family of origin.
- **Assessments:** Each type of personality assessment is unique and has value. Avoid using just one of these as the final word on personality styles.

Positive Uses of Personality Assessments and Love Languages
God uniquely created each of us. The goal of studying personality styles and love languages should be personal growth in our behavior and empathy, understanding, and appreciation toward those who are different from us.

- **Motivation:** The better we understand ourselves, the better we can identify what motivates our behavior. This can help us better utilize our positive traits and work on changing negative ones.
- **Relationships:** Understanding different personality styles and love languages can help not only our relationship with our spouse but also with our children, family members, friends, coworkers, and neighbors.
- **Many Normals:** As we study personality types, we realize all personality types are normal, and one type is not better than another. My personality type is normal for me, and my wife's personality type is normal for her.
- **Strengths and Weaknesses:** Each personality type has strengths and weaknesses. An emotionally and spiritually healthy person tends to exhibit the positive aspects of their personality type. Those who are struggling emotionally and spiritually may show more negative characteristics of their style.

- **Love Language:** We tend to demonstrate and give love to others in the way we prefer to receive love. Knowing the love language of our spouse, children, friends, and family members helps us to show love for them in their preferred love language.

ENNEAGRAM

The Enneagram describes nine personality types based on their core motivations, fears, and patterns of thinking, feeling, and behaving. The Enneagram can help people better understand themselves and others and improve their relationships and personal growth. Each of the nine Enneagram personality types is a normal personality style and has its own strengths and weaknesses (Cron & Stabile, 2016).

The following is a brief description of the nine Enneagram personality styles. We would encourage you to take the Enneagram test (https://www.truity.com/test/enneagram-personality-test). This free test takes approximately 15 minutes.

- **One – The Perfectionist (Reformer):** Ones place a lot of emphasis on following the rules and doing things correctly. Ones fear being imperfect and can be extremely strict with themselves and others.
- **Two – The Giver (Helper):** Twos want to be liked and find ways that they can be helpful to others so that they belong. Twos fear being unlovable.
- **Three – The Achiever:** Threes want to be successful and admired by other people and are very conscious of their public image. Threes fear failure and not being seen as valuable by other people.
- **Four – The Individualist:** Fours want to be unique and to experience deep, authentic emotions. Fours fear they are flawed and are overly focused on how they are different from other people.
- **Five – The Investigator:** Fives seek understanding and knowledge and are more comfortable with data than other people. Fives fear being overwhelmed by their own needs or the needs of other people.
- **Six – The Skeptic (Loyalist):** Sixes are preoccupied with security, seek safety, and like to be prepared for problems. Sixes fear being unprepared and unable to defend themselves from danger.
- **Seven – The Enthusiast:** Sevens want to have as much fun and adventure as possible and are easily bored. Sevens fear experiencing emotional pain, especially sadness, and actively seek to avoid it by staying busy.
- **Eight – The Challenger:** Eights see themselves as strong and powerful and seek to stand up for what they believe in. Eights fear to be powerless, so they focus on controlling their environment.

- **Nine – The Peacemaker:** Nines like to go with the flow and let the people around them set the agenda. Nines fear pushing people away by prioritizing their own needs, and they tend to be passive.

(Cron & Stabile, 2016; Truity.com, 2024)
See https://www.truity.com/blog/enneagram/9-types-enneagram for info about each Enneagram type. Click the "Read more about Enneagram #s" link for more detailed info about each number.

We recommend reading The Road Back to You by Ian Morgan Cron and Suzanne Stabile. This is an easy read and goes more into depth about the nine Enneagram personality styles, the three different triads, wings, and stress and security numbers.

THE FIVE LOVE LANGUAGES

The five love languages are how people express and receive love in relationships, according to Dr. Gary Chapman, who first introduced the concept in his book, The Five Love Languages: How to Express Heartfelt Commitment to Your Mate. Each love language has its own associated behaviors and preferences. The five love languages are words of ***affirmation, quality time, physical touch, acts of service, and receiving gifts*** (Chapman, 1992).

The following is a brief description of the five love languages. We would encourage you to take The Love Language Quiz (https://5lovelanguages.com/quizzes/love-language). This free test takes approximately 10 minutes.

- **Words of Affirmation:** Expressing love through verbal compliments, praise, and appreciation.
- **Quality Time:** Spending focused and uninterrupted time with your partner, doing meaningful activities, or having deep conversations.
- **Physical Touch:** Showing love through physical contact, such as hugging, kissing, holding hands, or cuddling.
- **Acts of Service:** Doing things for your partner that make their life easier or more comfortable, such as chores, errands, or favors.
- **Receiving Gifts:** Giving or receiving thoughtful and personal gifts that show you care and pay attention to your partner's needs and preferences.

(Chapman, 1992)
See https://5lovelanguages.com/learn for more detailed info about each of the five different love languages. We also recommend reading The Five Love Languages by Gary Chapman.

THINK ABOUT IT BY YOURSELF

If you haven't already, take both the Enneagram and The Love Languages assessments.
Enneagram: https://www.truity.com/test/enneagram-personality-test

The Love Languages: https://5lovelanguages.com/quizzes/love-language
Identify your top two categories for each of these tests and review the detailed information about each of these.

https://www.truity.com/blog/enneagram/9-types-enneagram: Click the "Read more about Enneagram #s" link for more detailed info about each number.

https://5lovelanguages.com/learn: Each love language has a short video

In what ways do the descriptions accurately reflect your personality styles and love languages? Are there some characteristics you disagree with?

Can you guess what your spouse's top two Enneagram numbers are? What positive and negative characteristics of these personality styles do they exhibit?

Can you guess what your spouse's top two love languages are? Are there things you regularly do that speak their love language?

———

The goal of studying personality styles and love languages should be growth in our own personal characteristics and behaviors and empathy, understanding, and appreciation towards those who are different from us.

———

TALK ABOUT IT AS A COUPLE

Share your guess of your spouse's top two love languages and the reason you think these are their love languages.

Share your guess of your spouse's top two Enneagram numbers and the reason you think these are their Enneagram numbers.

Share your top two love languages with your spouse. Describe how you feel when your spouse shows their love for you by using behavior that speaks your love language.

Share your top Enneagram number with your spouse. Describe what you've learned about yourself based on this Enneagram number.

After talking about both of your Enneagram numbers, talk about what you learned about your spouse based upon their Enneagram number.

DISCUSS IT AS A GROUP

Share your top two love languages with your group. Do you think your love languages have changed during your lifetime?

What are two or three things you have done or can do this week that show your love for your spouse in their love language?

Share your top Enneagram number among your group. Describe three or four characteristics of your number that best describe you.

Spend time reviewing and discussing the Healthy, Average, and Unhealthy aspects of your Enneagram number. (See https://www.truity.com/blog/enneagram/9-types-enneagram. Click the "Read more about Enneagram #s" link for more detailed info about each number). Do any of these descriptions particularly resonate with you?

Spend time reviewing and discussing the growth tips for your Enneagram number (see link and info above for growth tips for Enneagram numbers). What are some actions you can take to promote growth and emotional health in your life?

The better we understand our own and our spouse's unique personality and preferences, the easier it is to appreciate and celebrate the differences in our partner.

PRACTICE IT - BE INTENTIONAL

During a walk, date night, after the kids have gone to bed, or when you have 30 minutes or more interrupted time, discuss what you've learned about your partner regarding love languages and Enneagram numbers. Describe how you will try to speak your partner's love language better.

Review the Growth Tips of each of your Enneagram numbers. Talk about how you will help and support your spouse put into practice one or more of these tips.

Do another personality assessment, such as Meyers & Briggs, DISC, The Big Five, love styles, attachment styles, or spiritual pathways, and discuss your results.

DIGGING DEEPER

Chapman, G. (1992). The Five Love Languages: How to Express Heartfelt Commitment to Your Mate. Northfield Publishing.

Cron, I. M., & Stabile, S. (2016). The Road Back to You. InterVarsity Press.
Truity.com. (2024, 1 3). What Are the Nine Enneagram Types? Retrieved from Truity: https://www.truity.com/blog/enneagram/9-types-enneagram

SESSION 4

HAVING FUN AND REST

"Deep levels of trust, admiration, and respect should define every marriage." (pg. 33, FPL)

Do you remember how and when you fell in love? No two people fall in love without spending time together. ***Time*** is required to get to know one another because, without time, there is no knowledge. ***Time and knowledge are required for love to grow.***

In the same way that love begins, it continues. Without meaningful time together, a couple will forget why they love one another or actually stop loving one another.

Marriage is supposed to be fun. Not every day. Not in every season. But across the broad spectrum of living life together, marriage should be defined by joy, happiness, and gladness more often than it is dictated by struggle, frustration, and discontent. All are common elements of healthy relationships, but the positive characteristics should define the relationship far more than the negative ones.

In Session 2, we talked about the importance of ***friendship*** and ***trust***. To grow in friendship and trust, ***couples must spend time together,*** not only in the daily activities of life, but also doing ***fun activities.*** Most relationships begin with fun. The dating and honeymoon stage is playful. However, many couples ***slowly lose their sense of fun, adventure, and spontaneity*** as kids come along, careers develop, and the pressures of life replace the passions of new love. If a marriage is never fun, something is wrong.

MORE ABOUT TIME TOGETHER

Regularly, a couple comes to my office, and their marriage is in serious trouble. Their body language says it all. Sometimes, they are angry, sometimes dejected. Almost always, each has a mental narrative of what has gone wrong. They talk about how "life has been crazy," "we are constantly running a thousand different directions," and "work is demanding." They might mention how tired they have become. **But they seldom admit, or they fail to see, the root of the issue----—they have stopped spending meaningful time together.** Is it any surprise that a couple who never spends time together, apart from trying to manage day-to-day life, no longer feels a deep emotional connection and love for one another?

You Don't Have to Spend Time Together Every Day

While the newly married and empty nesters might have the opportunity to spend time together every day, that is not the story of those who are raising children. The demands of life are just too great.

- If you have children and careers, *quality time with your spouse is limited.*
- A couple doesn't have to spend time together every day to be successful.
- *We can thrive* without hours being spent together daily.

You Do Have to Spend Time Together on a Regular Basis

The longer a couple goes without spending time together, the greater their risk of love's feelings fading, disagreements becoming more destructive, and an affair to look more tempting.

- A couple must spend *regular time together.* It doesn't have to be every day.

- Unless a couple *intentionally* tries to have *meaningful time together,* it will not happen.

- *Recognize life's demands and distractions,* and *intentionally plan* meaningful time with our spouse.

You Can Find Time for One Another

Spending time together doesn't take a lot of money or demand a large chunk of time. But it does demand *intention* and *attention.* Love requires *time.* To the extent we choose to spend time with our spouses, we will likely feel love for them.

- *Stop* during the morning routine, *look* each other in the eye, and *talk* for two or three minutes
- Take a break from work and *text* one another.
- *Turn off the television* and have a meaningful conversation.
- Take a *walk*.
- Get a babysitter and go to the park or go for a drive.
- Have *lunch* together.

MORE ABOUT HAVING FUN

One of the most common relationship mistakes is assuming that having fun together doesn't matter. We think it's nice to have, but life isn't just about good times, so *we fail to prioritize fun* within our marriages. Yet, *having fun together does matter.* While it's not the foundational reason why marriage was designed, it is a vital element to connecting with the one we love.

What Fun Does

It helps us endure hardship.
- People who suffer well have an *ability to see the good* even during hardships.
- We laugh, in part, to help us *get through hard times.*
- When the fun factor of our marriage decreases, we lose our ability to endure difficult

It reminds us we aren't alone.
- Laughter is rarely in response to a joke. For one day, pay attention to when and why people laugh.
- While it's true that we laugh when something is funny, we usually laugh to *acknowledge* others, *connect* with them, and *show* we are not a threat.
- Having fun in a relationship *reminds us that we are not alone.* We have someone else who is for us and with us.

It positively impacts our kids.
- Few things are more important than for our kids to *see us enjoying one another's*
- In a world that rarely gives a positive picture of marriage, our children need to see that their *mom and dad love each other and have fun together.*
- *Prioritizing time together and having fun* will help our children view marriage as a positive aspect of life, and they will most likely emulate this in their own marriages.

Why Fun Leaves

It's one thing to know that playfulness in marriage matters, but it's another thing to understand what causes it to disappear. By recognizing what destroys fun in marriage, we can be better equipped to avoid those elements. Here are 5 things that take the fun out of marriage:

Distrust
- Enjoyment can only happen when we feel *safe.*
- The absence of fun in a relationship is typically a *symptom of distrust.*
- *Humor, laughter,* and *playfulness* all require a *base level of trust.* When distrust is present, fun is not.

Disrespect

- *Playfulness* is born of *equality.*
- When we feel disrespected by our spouse, *we do not feel like their equal* and cannot enjoy time with them.
- *Lack of respect* prevents us from having fun.

Pressure

- The higher our stress level, the less likely we are to *see the good in others and enjoy life and relationships.*
- When we feel pressure, *our vision narrows,* and we focus on the source of the pressure.
- While it's fair to expect seasons where we are pressed by various issues (debt, conflict, busyness of life), we must *be diligent to avoid unnecessary stressors* and navigate those things that we can't avoid.

Time

- *Fun demands time.*
- Many couples never have enough time together to enjoy their interaction.
- Only after we've spent enough time together to cover the big issues will we have *enough time to simply enjoy one another.*

Habits

- When a couple gets into the habit of not having fun, they will likely *continue that habit until something changes.*
- When we apathetically accept negative patterns of behavior, it will *destroy any sense of fun* in our marriage.
- Healthy couples make enjoyment habitual. They intentionally find ways to have fun.

Why Fun Returns

While many actions and activities can increase the enjoyment we experience in marriage, several specific actions define fun relationships.

Be Intentional

- Without intention, time will erode our joy. We don't naturally drift toward positive mindsets or behaviors.
- Recognize that *fun is an intended aspect of a healthy relationship.*
- Choose actions that will i*ncrease the likelihood of good times.*

Be Adventurous

- Some people are more *adventurous,* while others are more *cautious.*
- To increase the joy in our marriage, we should *occasionally step outside of our comfort zones.*
- One of the best ways to have more fun in a relationship is to *do something new together.*

Be Playful

- *Playfulness is a mindset;* it's an appropriate attempt to lighten the mood even during difficult times.
- We should attempt to l*augh, bring humor,* or *create games* to better carry a tough load.
- Life is short and hard; we should s*eek the good* and *enjoy* as much of it as we can.

Be Gracious

- To the extent that we feel undeserving of the good we have been given, we will *extend grace to others.*
- Entitlement kills enjoyment, but grace makes it thrive.
- We must give grace to each other when things don't go as expected.

Some Final Thoughts About Time Together and Having Fun

- Healthy relationships are characterized by *playfulness, good cheer,* and *enjoyment.*
- Marriage isn't solely about having fun, but it should be *a natural byproduct of two people who love each other well.*
- While some seasons will be defined by great struggle, *the long arch of a relationship should be viewed fondly.*
- Even difficult times can be easier when a couple *can see the good and share it with one another.*

THINK ABOUT IT BY YOURSELF

How would you describe your marriage regarding time spent with one another? Flooded (too much), saturated (just right), or drought (not enough)? Why?

What relationships do you have individually and as a couple that are good for your marriage?

Do you or your spouse have relationships that have a negative influence on your relationship?

What do you enjoy most about your spouse?

What fun activities and adventures did you do with your spouse when you were dating or in your early marriage years? Do you still do some of these activities?

What fun activities do you enjoy doing with your spouse now?

TALK ABOUT IT WITH YOUR SPOUSE

Discuss the amount and quality of time you spend together as a couple.

What are some boundaries you have set (or should set) to ensure uninterrupted conversation without interference by technology or other factors?

Determine one habit you could form as a couple to ensure quality time spent together.

Describe a truly fun time while dating or in your marriage. Do you still regularly do fun things together?

What routine do you have as a couple when you leave each other and when you return to each other? Are there habits (a kiss, extended hug, etc.) that you could develop?

Describe one date night that sounds fun. Set a time to create that date.

To grow in friendship and trust, **_couples must spend time together,_** not only in the daily activities of life, but also **_doing activities that are fun._**

DISCUSS IT AS A GROUP

What are some of your best practices to spend quality time together?

Have there been seasons in your life that have been more challenging to carve out time together? How did you make an adjustment to find more time together?

Describe one of your favorite activities or adventures you've had with your spouse. Are you still intentionally planning and doing fun activities together?

How has having fun together as a couple positively influenced those around you (children, family, friends, neighbors, coworkers)?

How is a lack of play sometimes a sign that distrust is present in the relationship? How can developing trust lead to more playfulness?

What are some ways to grow your sense of gratitude as a tool to increase the fun in your marriage?

PRACTICE IT - BE INTENTIONAL

Plan a day and time each week when you spend 30 or more minutes together without technology or other interruptions. Go for a walk, go to dinner or lunch, go for a drive or bike ride where you can talk and have uninterrupted time with each other.

Plan a new and fun activity or adventure you can do together this month.

DIGGING DEEPER

Friends, Partners, and Lovers by Kevin A. Thompson. Chapter 3, "No Wonder You Don't Love Each Other," and Chapter 4, "The Most Overlooked Characteristic of Marriage."

SESSION 5

PARTNERSHIP AND RESPECT

"At its best, marriage is the partnership of two equals who use their strengths in different areas for the mutual benefit of the couple." (pg. 96, FPL)

At the altar, the bride and groom promise to love one another. It's the formation of a unique relationship where a couple vows to become *friends, partners,* and *lovers.* At its best, marriage is the gift of knowing someone will always *walk by your side, have your back*, and *see you eye to eye.* Living life with a partner is a great gift.

But just as I often stand before couples making these vows, I sit before couples on the brink of divorce. They aren't friends because they have drifted from each other's side. They aren't partners who have each other's backs because they are too worried the other might stab them in the back. *For a partnership to thrive, it must be based on a foundation of trust and respect.*

The absence of respect is a key indicator of a marriage in trouble. As a pastor, one of the most heartbreaking sights I see is when a couple no longer recognizes the most basic level of human dignity in one another. Skepticism and hurt blind their eyes to such an extent that they are incapable of giving any respect to one another.

An absence of respect kills one's heart. No couple intends to get to that point, yet far too many end up in my office unable to see the person next to them as someone who deserves to be treated decently, spoken to properly, and valued as a spouse. *Yet, where respect exists, there is hope.*

MORE ABOUT PARTNERSHIP

Is Your Spouse for You?

If you cannot quickly and confidently answer that question, you have a major problem. It may not be immediately fatal, but it is a growing cancer in your relationship and partnership. Most individuals fail to positively answer the question for one of two reasons:

1. **Their spouse can't say they are for them.** For some, there is no doubt or pretending. Both parties know they are not for each other. *They are all about themselves and nothing else.* If the well-being of the other person happens to run parallel with their personal well-being, that's a bonus, but generally, one spouse uses the other for personal gain.

2. **Their spouse's actions do not prove that they are for them.** In some relationships, the husband or wife says they are for their spouse, but their actions don't back up their words. In this case, what they say doesn't matter. *Actions prove the reality of words.* If your spouse doesn't act in your best interest, they are not for you. (Note: We can be for our spouse, but not for the bad choices they are making. Recognize the difference.)

Are You for Your Spouse?

While it's important to know that our spouse is for us, *the first step to a good marriage and partnership is making sure we are for our spouse and that our spouse knows, feels, and sees us being for them.* It's easy to know if we feel our spouse has our back or not. But we shouldn't be so quick to assume our husband or wife knows we have theirs. The following are some ways to show it.

- You want your spouse's success maybe even more than they desire it.
- You celebrate their wins without any semblance of jealousy.
- You regularly and honestly speak words of affirmation to your spouse.
- You feel joy when someone compliments your spouse.
- You speak highly and positively (even brag) about your spouse to others.
- You don't speak negatively about your spouse to others.
- You regularly watch out for them and try to compensate for their weaknesses without them noticing.
- You ask them daily, "What is one thing I can take off your plate today?"

MORE ABOUT RESPECT

Do not ignore an absence of respect in your marriage. *A good marriage is built on respect.* We should continually look for tangible ways to show respect to our partners.

A lack of respect leads to contempt. In his book, *7 Principles for Making Marriage Work*, John Gottman names contempt as one of the Four Horseman of the Apocalypse, which can destroy marriage. Often cloaked in sarcasm or cynicism, *contempt shows we do not respect our spouse.*

When we fail to respect our spouses, we are communicating that *we do not value them*. Many people make the false dichotomy that men need respect, and women need love. *The truth is both men and women need love and respect.* The following are suggestions to develop and nourish respect for our partner.

Stop Disrespecting

- Stop *talking down* to your spouse.
- Stop *feeling superior* to them.
- Stop overestimating your value and underestimating their value.
- Answer when you are spoken to in a voice that is loud enough to be heard but quiet enough so you aren't yelling.
- Pay attention to the *tone* and the *intent of your words*
- Stop *looking at your phone* when your spouse is talking.

Show Respect

- Practice *gratefulness.* Say "thank you" and "please."
- Recognize when your request requires something from your partner and communicate your awareness of that fact.
- Assist your spouse in accomplishing their *goals* and *dreams*.
- Communicate when you feel respected by your spouse.
- Ask your spouse what makes them feel most respected by you.

Fixate on Your Spouse's Strengths

- Focus on their successes.
- Vocalize your support.
- Overlook minor flaws.
- Find the good.
- Believe that your spouse is for you.

The easiest way to maintain respect is to focus on your spouse's positive qualities. **Disrespect** often results from **overthinking our spouse's negative qualities** to the exclusion of their positive ones. While we shouldn't deny the faults of our spouses, we also shouldn't fixate on them. **Focus on their strengths, and respect will grow.**

I've never seen a successful marriage that wasn't built on **true respect** and **admiration** for one another.

THINK ABOUT IT BY YOURSELF

What are three strengths you greatly admire about your spouse?

What are some ways you show (not just tell) your spouse that you love them and are for them?

List three or more ways that you show respect to and for your spouse.

List three or more things that would make you feel disrespected by your spouse. Does your spouse ever engage in those activities? If so, give an example.

What are some things your spouse does that demonstrate they are for you?

SESSION 5: PARTNERSHIP AND RESPECT

What are some things your spouse does that demonstrate respect toward you?

Is there anything that holds you back from fully loving and supporting your spouse?

TALK ABOUT IT WITH YOUR SPOUSE

Describe a time in which you felt loved and supported by your spouse.
What made you feel that way?

Do you feel like your spouse is fully for you? Describe to your spouse what it would look like if you had your spouse's full support.

Is there anything that holds you back from fully loving and supporting your spouse?

Describe to your spouse a time when you felt disrespected. Did you let your spouse know how you felt at the time?

Describe to your spouse a time when they showed you respect. How did that make you feel?

The first step to a good marriage and partnership is ensuring we are for our spouse and that our spouse knows, feels, and sees us being for them.

DISCUSS IT AS A GROUP

Discuss what it means to you to be in a partnership with your spouse. What are some tangible ways you are a good partner to your spouse? Are there areas where you can be a better partner?

One evidence of respect is being able to be influenced by the other person. How does your spouse positively influence you?

Describe a time in which you felt greatly respected by your spouse. What made you feel respected?

Have there been times in your relationship where you have felt disrespected? Describe how you worked through this issue.

Describe some of the ways you intentionally show respect to your partner.

PRACTICE IT - BE INTENTIONAL

Choose one way you will better show love and support to your spouse this week.

When out for a walk, dinner, or alone together, ask your spouse about their goals and dreams.

Ask what you can do to help them accomplish one or more of these goals and dreams.
Write a note, email, or lengthy text telling your spouse one thing you respect about them and why.

DIGGING DEEPER

Friends, Partners, and Lovers by Kevin A. Thompson. Chapter 3, "No Wonder You Don't Love Each Other," and Chapter 4, "The Most Overlooked Characteristic of Marriage."

7 Principles for Making Marriage Work, John Gottman

SESSION 6

MONEY

"Whenever we fail to live by good financial principles, we are doing more than just straining our relationships; we are also suffocating our dreams." (pg.142, FPL)

Money is one of the top five reasons people divorce. Show me a couple who can't get on the same page financially, and I'll show you a relationship that will always face difficulties. Yet when a couple **understands one another** and **works together regarding money,** they can avoid many financial pitfalls experienced in marriage.

One of the greatest struggles regarding money is that the word means different things to different people. Until we recognize this truth, we could regularly be saying the same thing to one another without realizing we mean radically different things.

What does money mean to you?

Security, pleasure, power, and **opportunity** are things that first come to mind regarding money. Consider: if a wife sees money as an **opportunity** and her husband sees it first as **security**, what are the possible arguments or misunderstandings that could happen when they discuss money?

Knowing what money means to you and to your spouse is an essential first step to getting in harmony regarding finances. And remember, **having different viewpoints of what money means is ripe with opportunity for growth** if we can understand, appreciate, and be influenced by our spouse's view. Failing to understand we see money differently is a recipe for frustration.

MONEY AND COMMUNICATION

While every couple needs to learn to handle money properly, the first step is learning how to communicate about it. ***What many people see as a money problem is actually an inability to communicate about money.*** When wives and husbands learn to have productive conversations regarding their finances, there is little limit to what they can achieve. Yet talking about money is often difficult for the following reasons:

Money talks often feel personal and judgmental.

- Because our meaning of money often comes from our family of origin, seeing money differently feels like an attack on our heritage.
- We often overestimate how well others have their financial house in order, so disagreements make us feel uniquely struggling or broken.
- **Solution: *Approach the problem as "us" against the problem rather than husband vs. wife.***

Money talks often expose inequality in knowledge or income.

- If one or both partners are insecure regarding money, these discussions can create deeper insecurity.
- If equal respect is absent, one partner might attempt to dominate the discussion or force their desired outcome.
- Occasionally, the spouse who earns a higher paycheck feels they should have more say in what happens with the money.
- **Solution: *Respect differences in your opinions about money and remember that budgeting and financial goals are things we work together to accomplish.***

Money talks often spark emotion.

- Money talks are often not about money. They become emotional when we fail to see the real issues—things like security, opportunity, equality, and respect.
- Many couples don't talk about money until there are problems, and sometimes well past the first presentation of those problems. Higher stress means more emotional talks.
- **Solution: *Have regular "business" meetings where financial issues are discussed. Don't wait for problems to escalate.***
- **Solution: *If discussions become emotional, pause and ask yourself what lies underneath the emotion. Deal with that issue. Remember, it's often about more than money.***

Money talks often lack resolution.

- Many couples fight about money but never change any behavior.
- When individuals are unwilling to change behaviors, they repeatedly have the same conversations.
- **Solution:** *If you repeatedly struggle with an issue, seek the help of a financial planner or another couple you trust.*

MORE ABOUT MONEY

Give, Save, Spend

Giving, saving, and spending are at the heart of a wise financial strategy. We handle money in those three ways and in that specific order. First, we give because God gave to us. Second, we save, recognizing we can influence the future. Finally, we spend to manage our household and our lives.

Give

- We give as acts of ***obedience*** and ***thankfulness*** to God and to remind ourselves that everything we have received is a gift.
- ***Giving is an intentional act to*** help save us from materialism.
- We give intentionally, sacrificially, and ***spontaneously.***
- Out of ***gratitude*** toward Jesus and others, we seek to live a ***life of generosity.***

Save

- Saving reminds us that we can ***live off less than what we earn.***
- We save to have more ***influence*** over our future.
- Saving reminds us that delayed gratification is a better ***pathway to our desired life.***
- Saving is one step toward ***making each other's dreams come true.***

Spend

- Budgeting is essential to helping us spend within the resources we have received.
- Having already given saved, and budgeted, we spend without guilt or reservation.
- We spend on necessities and things that bring us joy.

Debt

There are few things as stressful in a marriage as debt. While debt can be leveraged for good (it can get you home, allow for education, and present a business opportunity), it should be used in limited ways and with a keen awareness of the damage it can do in marriage.

- ***Deciding to eliminate debt can unify a couple*** in a common task and set them free of one of the great stressors of marriage.

- Moving beyond living paycheck to paycheck is a form of *freedom* that every couple should experience.
- Many *good resources* exist to help with debt elimination and budgeting.

Dreams

Couples often need help to recognize the correlation between spending and dreaming. When a husband and wife are financially wise, they create a future where both can *pursue and experience their dreams.* Yet when they foolishly spend money without thinking about the future, they unknowingly hinder their ability to *pursue new ventures, experience bucket-list dreams, or give generously to others.*

- Spending carelessly *hinders the ability to accomplish dreams.*
- *Budgeting* and *saving* don't sound sexy, but there is a direct correlation between a couple's level of stress and their sexual satisfaction.
- Saving doesn't seem fun, but when a couple wisely orders their financial house, *they can be more spontaneous* with trips, indulgence purchases, and generosity.
- Financial wisdom isn't about ruining the fun of today; it's about *creating an opportunity* for tomorrow to be as limitless as possible.

THE NUMBER ONE MONEY RULE

The number one rule of money for couples is complete financial transparency, except for meaningful surprises. For a short season, a husband or wife can do something with money to have a good surprise for their spouse. But that's it. *Surprises, not secrets.*

Every other scenario requires complete *transparency built on trust and respect.* We must show one another that we will unselfishly handle money. We give, save, and spend through the lens of "us" and not just "me." This doesn't mean one partner should go over the spending of the other with a fine tooth comb. In many budgets, each partner may have some discretionary money to spend however they wish. But with the big picture in mind, there are no secrets. No slush funds. No hidden golf money or secret credit card or undisclosed loan. Full financial transparency is essential to a healthy and thriving marriage.

- *All money is our money:* There is no "his money" or "her money." It's not "his paycheck" or "her account." It all belongs to us.
- Each person is entitled to know (and have a say about) where the money goes.
- As we seek to build the life and marriage we desire, financial unity is critical.

In unique situations, it might be necessary to have separate accounts. If one partner struggles with financial discipline, a separate account could be set up with a regular stipend going into that account. But even in that scenario, everything should happen in the open. In most circumstances, every account should be a joint account, with each person having full access to all the necessary information.

THINK ABOUT IT BY YOURSELF

What does money mean to you? Which of these four words best describe it—security, pleasure, power, or opportunity?

How was money discussed in your family of origin? Was it a point of contention? Was it ignored?

If left unchecked, how could greed or materialism negatively impact your ability to be a good husband or wife?
From where or whom did you learn about money? In retrospect, was that a wise source?

Is there any financial secret you have kept from your spouse that you need to disclose?

What are three dreams or bucket-list experiences you would like to have?
Have you told them to your spouse?

In marriage, all money is our money. There is no such thing as his check or my check, his account or my account. It all belongs to us.

TALK ABOUT IT WITH YOUR SPOUSE

Take turns sharing with your spouse what money was like in your family of origin. Was it tight? Was there plenty? How was it discussed?

Discuss your core meanings of money. Are they the same? Do they differ?

If money became a point of contention in your relationship, what's the most likely way for that to express itself in your relationship?

Share two of your dreams with your spouse, and together, brainstorm one action step you could take to get closer to experiencing that dream.

What is your current net worth? How much debt? How many assets? Are you both clear on exactly where you stand?

What does "enough" money look like for you? What do you want to experience or achieve?

DISCUSS IT AS A GROUP

Why do you think many lottery winners end up regretting that they won?

If you were given a large sum of money, what's the scenario in your relationship where that could hurt your marriage?

What's the scenario in which you might be tempted to break the number one financial rule? Why?

Why did Jesus have us pray for our daily bread? How does that impact our view of money?

What do money talks look like in your relationship? What's one thing you would like to see improved regarding communication and money?

What is the dollar amount that requires both spouses permission before spending?

Are you moving toward making your dreams come true or just surviving week to week? Why?

PRACTICE IT - BE INTENTIONAL

Have a business meeting. Prepare a one sheet with your financial status—all accounts, amount of debt, etc. Discuss where you are and where you would like to be.

Pick one area regarding finances where you want to learn more. Read a book on that topic and discuss it with your spouse.

Schedule a date night in a bookstore where the only topics allowed to be discussed are future dreams. Save the day-to-day discussion for another time. Brainstorm what your life could be like in the future. Peruse travel sections, careers, and hobbies to get ideas.

DIGGING DEEPER

Friends, Partners, and Lovers by Kevin A. Thompson. Chapter 6, "Marry a Partner, Not a Child," and Chapter 10, "How to Make Her Dreams Come True."

The Total Money Makeover by Dave Ramsey.

SESSION 7

WORK

"The equality of the couple is not determined by salary.
It is determined by their equal work, passion, and contribution." (pg.144, FPL)

Work is not a necessary evil. It is an essential aspect of what it means to be human. We were all created to work. When a person refuses to leverage their God-given talents and resources, expending their energy for the achievement of a goal, they suffer negative consequences. When we fail to work, the energy meant to be used through us is turned on us.

Work doesn't just mean a job for which we get paid. Work includes **career, household tasks,** and ways we **volunteer** our time. While neither spouse may spend significant time at all three, each must be considered in how they use their time, energy, and resources.

Work brings a **variety of benefits.** But just as money means different things to different people, **so does work.** Understanding what matters most to you and your spouse is a key element to understanding the impact of work on marriage. Ideally, our marriage will have a positive impact on our work, and our work will have a positive impact on our marriage. But marriage and work can compete against each other, hindering both.

A couple who learns to **leverage work for the well-being of their relationship** avoids many common pitfalls of marriage and is strengthened by the benefits of a meaningful work life.

CAREER, HOUSEHOLD, AND VOLUNTEER

When we consider work, we think of it in at least three distinct forms—*career, household,* and *volunteer.* Each plays a role in a healthy home.

Effort is a major contributor to marital satisfaction. But if we do not place proper effort in the right areas, our marriage will suffer. Proper emphasis on work and rest, effort, and connection are vital for a successful marriage.

- *Work too little,* and you are failing to be a partner in the relationship. Your spouse will feel the weight of everything on their shoulders. The relationship will devolve into a parent/child dynamic.

- *Work too much,* and your spouse will feel isolated. Even as you think you are pulling your weight, they will wonder what the weight is being pulled for. The relationship will devolve into a roommate scenario.

Career

For some, a career is just a means to make money, but for most, it is much more. **We were created to work; a career is one outlet for expressing that work.** Many wrongly associate careers more with men than women, even though women often rank their careers as a higher priority for life satisfaction than men do. (66% to 59%, according to John Gottman).

There is a strong correlation with satisfaction in marriage and work. *The better one's marriage, the more likely they will be happy at work. The happier one is at work, the more likely their marriage is satisfying.* Rather than seeing work and home as a competition, we should view them as complementing one another. In both, we are partners as we work together and cheer each other on in our individual pursuits.

Career and Money

- While work and money are not synonymous, we have bills to pay. Our jobs must be sufficient for the lifestyle we desire, or we must adjust our lifestyles to our income.

- *Job satisfaction is more important than wealth.* Being wealthy is not necessarily detrimental to marital satisfaction, but chasing wealth at the expense of relationships prevents life satisfaction. *Finding a job that is both satisfying and financially sustainable is key.*

- For most, the one-career life is over. Since you are likely to have multiple jobs and careers throughout your life, *it's essential to always save money so you have flexibility if a job transition is necessary.*

Career and Time

- *Time together as a couple is non-negotiable.* You can't have a satisfying marriage without it. No matter how demanding a job is, *you must make time for your spouse and family.*

- *Work schedules should be taken into consideration before accepting a job.* If your two schedules are not compatible, it will be difficult to stay connected.

Career and Sacrifice

- *Seasons occur in which one spouse sacrifices for the dreams of the other.* The sacrifice must be seen and appreciated.

- *Career success should be viewed as a byproduct of teamwork,* not one person's success.

- *Sacrifice can't be one-sided.* If the wife repeatedly puts off her dreams for her husband's career, at some point, the husband must take a backseat for the wife's dreams to be pursued.

- Notice: *Being a workaholic is often a method of avoidance.* We must face why we turn to work rather than connecting with those close to us.

Work/Life Balance

- Balance is a poor metaphor. *Rarely is everything 50/50.* At times, family will be more demanding. In seasons, work will require much. Don't think in terms of balance.

- *Work/Life rhythm is a better mindset.* Create patterns of work, rest, connection, rejuvenation, and life.

- Notice: *Our spouses and families must see, not just hear, that they are more important to us than work.*

Household

While a career is essential, *managing household duties is often a significant source of frustration.* Seventy-five years ago, men had careers, women did the household chores, and there was little debate. However, as women entered the workforce, many men never picked up their share of the household duties. This led to great strife and is not a sustainable model. While the workload may vary in different seasons, *both partners should be fully involved in running the house.*

Division of Labor

- The expectation is equal effort at differing tasks. *Determine who does what by when.*
- We each have leadership in various tasks, but that doesn't put that job on us completely. *We still assist each other in all things.*

- *Have a quarterly or annual review* to ensure too much hasn't fallen on one spouse.
- *Switching responsibilities occasionally* is an excellent way to check the workload balance.
- *Teamwork, support for each other, and communication* are key to creating a healthy household environment.

Seasons of Change

- Household demands change with the seasons of life. *Don't assume that what worked last year will work this year.* Talk about it.
- People change. Just because one spouse enjoys doing a task today doesn't mean they will like it tomorrow. *Continually communicate and renegotiate who does what.*
- Remember, time is money. *Choose which duties you will pay to have done and which will be done by the family.*

Parenting

- *Avoid the good cop/bad cop model.* Both parents should enforce the rules.
- Rather than making judgments at the moment, having a basic set of household rules with pre-stated consequences lessens the stress for parents and children.
- Many couples experience more disagreements in parenting than in any other area. *See the differences as an opportunity for growth.*

Volunteer

The third key element of work is often forgotten about in marriage. *Working outside the home without getting paid is a valuable venture for self, society, and marriage.* Too often, spouses devalue non-paid work, which fails to recognize the passion of a spouse, the contribution to society, and the calling of God found in the cultural mandate to be caretakers of what we have been given.

- *Volunteering should be accepted* and expected both individually and as a couple.
- Kids teams need to be coached. Homerooms need volunteers. Churches are dependent on volunteers.
- *Create a culture of service both in and out of the home.* Finding a place to serve together can significantly impact a couple and the community.
- Just like a career, we must ensure that we don't use volunteering as a way to avoid our marriage or other responsibilities.
- *Volunteering models a life of selflessness* to our children, family, friends, and neighbors.

MORE ABOUT WORK

Work as Vocation

In Christian thought, work (whether paid or unpaid, in the home or out) is considered a **vocation.** Each person is created by God, given unique gifts, and expected to use those gifts for the well-being of God's creation. **Work isn't just survival; it's service.**

- When we see **work as a vocation,** it opens a whole new opportunity to **display our belief in God, live His commandments** in various settings, and **act in faith.**

- This perspective should **impact not only why we work but also how we work.** We will not see a sacred/secular divide. Instead, we will see an **integral tie between worship and work.**

- **Seeing work as a vocation makes every moment and action meaningful.** There is no mundane task. Feeding a child, running a nation, or doing a life-saving surgery are all viewed as vital and valued.

Cognitive Labor (aka Mental Load)

Cognitive labor, also known as **Mental Load,** is the mental work it takes to maintain a household. This type of work often goes unnoticed in relationships but is an essential part of the division of household labor. Consider the following:

- Groceries don't just have to be purchased; thought must be given to what groceries are needed.

- We don't just have to take our kids to the dentist; someone must consider when they need to go, what dentist they will see, and call to make the appointment.

- We don't just need to get Mom a birthday card; someone must remember when her birthday is.

Cognitive labor often takes an unseen toll on a relationship. The challenge of the mental load is twofold:

- It's **unseen yet taxin**g and leads to exhaustion.

- It is often **not evenly distributed** in a relationship. This inequality leads to **burnout, anxiety, depression, sleeplessness**, and **unhealthy coping.**

Recognizing Cognitive Labor

The consequences of *cognitive labor* are rarely sourced back to *mental load* because it is a labor that is unseen. *We must intentionally recognize this vital aspect of work.*

- *Cognitive labor* must be considered when determining the total division of labor.
- Don't just look at who does what; also *consider who remembers what.* Remembering is an essential part of the process of work.
- *Saying, "Why didn't you ask for help?" does not change the mental load.*
- *Ask your spouse for help when needed (and before you get frustrated).*
- *Proactively and intentionally look for ways to help your spouse* and regularly ask your spouse if they need help.

THINK ABOUT IT BY YOURSELF

What does work mean to you? Of the following words, identify the three that resonate the most with you regarding work: money, purpose, self-worth, contribution to society, expression of creativity, social connection, and source of growth.

How was work viewed in your family of origin? How were your mom and dad different regarding work? How has your family of origin impacted your view of work?

If you were lazy, how would it express itself in your life? Would you be lazier toward work or lazier toward relationships?

Identify someone who you think is successful in work and marriage. What makes them that way? What decisions have they made over their lives to accomplish success?

Is there any place in your relationship where you feel you aren't carrying enough responsibility?

Is there any place you feel taken advantage of?

Are you doing what you always wanted, or do you have a dream job you still desire to achieve?

———————

When we see work as a vocation, it opens a whole new opportunity to display our belief in God, live his commandments in various settings, and act in faith, believing He will use our actions for the greater good.

———————

TALK ABOUT IT WITH YOUR SPOUSE

Compare the three words you chose regarding work with those your spouse chose. What's the same? What's different? How does that impact discussions about work?

How do your families of origin differ regarding careers, housework, and volunteering? Is there something you want to emulate from them? Anything you want to avoid?

Could the two of you work together? If so, what would you do? If not, what is the ideal job for each of you?

What are some things you could do better to ensure neither spouse is carrying too much of the cognitive load?

If you have kids, identify the main areas in which you have different parenting expectations.

DISCUSS IT AS A GROUP

What's your greatest point of tension regarding work in your marriage—career, household, or volunteering?

What would be your bucket list career? If money was no option, what would you do with your time?

How does seeing work as a vocation change our perspective of what we do?

How does parenting change the dynamic of work and career? How can we ensure that we are on the same page?

What season of life are you in, and what are two things you can do now to prepare for the season you are headed toward?

Why is volunteering/serving such an underutilized tool by couples, and what's one way we can start serving together?

PRACTICE IT - BE INTENTIONAL

Take one week and switch every job/responsibility outside your professional work. See how much work is on your spouse and determine if you are sharing the workload.

Make a date and only talk about career goals, dreams of businesses you could start, or jobs you would do if money was no object.

Identify one responsibility that you hate. For one month, pay someone to do that task. After the month, determine if that is money you could spend regularly.

DIGGING DEEPER

Friends, Partners, and Lovers by Kevin A. Thompson. Chapter 6 "Marry a Partner, Not a Child."

Every Good Endeavor by Timothy Keller (New York: Penguin Books, 2014)

SESSION 8

COMMUNICATION AND CONFLICT

"Differences are both the source of our greatest frustration
and the place of our greatest potential." (pg. 97, FPL)

Communication is the most reported source of struggles within a relationship when I ask couples about their marriage. On one hand, this shows the importance of communication and how every couple can benefit from improved communication. On the other hand, communication is rarely the true problem in marriage; it's most often a symptom of some other struggle.

A difficult aspect of communication is that it's something we all do and assume we are good at. Therefore, every problem is a sign that our partner either isn't understanding correctly or needs to communicate their ideas better. The truth is **no one is good at communication.**
The most significant difference between healthy and unhealthy couples when it comes to communication is not that one couple is great at it, and the other struggles. It's that one understands the difficulty of communication while the other does not.

Conflict is often linked to communication. It can create bad communication while also resulting from bad communication. While some conflict can be avoided through wise decision-making, humility, and learning important skills, no relationship is without conflict. Healthy relationships occasionally have more conflict because they do not deny or suppress issues. Instead, they discuss differences, recognize threats to the relationship, and confront struggles before they become significant problems.

ASSERTIVE COMMUNICATION

There are four major types of communication. They can be divided into secure (assertive) and insecure (passive, aggressive, and passive-aggressive). The goal is to create a relationship where we consistently communicate assertively. Yet, we all will have times in which we slip into non-secure communication. We should recognize these patterns and be willing to learn new assertive behaviors.

Non-Secure
Passive

- Downplays needs and desires. Hopes the other person will figure out what we want.
- Avoids conflict by pretending to agree with the spouse.
- Speaks in quiet tones, sometimes difficult for the other person to hear so that they can deny what they said.
- Directs eyes away from the other person, finding safety in disconnection.
- Quickly yields to the other person's viewpoint or plan.

Aggressive

- Demands one's way and demeans the ideas/feelings of others.
- Dominates the conversation. Speaks over the other.
- Refuses to listen to others or to seriously consider their viewpoint.
- Belittles others, not leaving room for disagreement.
- Uses body language to intimidate and speaks loudly.

Passive-Aggressive

- Deceives others as being kind but actually is self-centered.
- Denies the hostility underneath their communication.
- Words and body language don't match.
- Procrastinates to protest and get their way.
- Gives backhanded compliments or uses sarcasm not to be funny but to make their point.

Secure

Assertive

- Declares needs, wants, and desires with clarity.
- Respects the personhood of the other and their right to have differing opinions or desires.
- Makes eye contact and talks directly to the other person.
- Speaks clearly—neither in quiet tones nor with harshness.
- Seeks feedback and is open to discussion.

The Goal of Communication

Two decades ago, the thought in marriage therapy was that if couples could learn to communicate, it would solve their marriage difficulties. So, therapists taught couples to use "I" statements, stay calm, fight fairly, and communicate well. Yet divorce rates didn't change. Why not? Because while good communication is useful, it is never an end in itself. ***Connection is more important than communication.*** When used to assist connection, communication is a useful tool. Communicating well without connecting with each other accomplishes very little.

The goal is connection. We should communicate wisely, but we are ultimately trying to see and be seen, soothe and be soothed, feel safe, and make our partner feel safe.

Five Communication Hacks

1. Explain the Gap: When trying to communicate unmet expectations, a clear way to do so is to say, "I expected A, but I got B... Help me understand," or "You said A, but you did B... Help me understand." This simple process of stating what you thought or wanted to happen, as opposed to what actually happened, communicates your confusion clearly. ***By saying, "Help me understand," you let the other person know that you understand there could be valid reasons why it didn't happen.*** This approach honors the other person and allows them to explain their side of the story.

2. Refuse to speak or read between the lines: Say what you mean and mean what you say. **Refrain from holding** *each other accountable for what you failed to communicate.* Let frustration teach you how to communicate better instead of assuming your spouse should know better. Train your spouse to understand who you are, what you believe, and what you desire.

3. Ignore the first verbal jab: Communication can quickly become tense when we feel threatened or attacked. ***When the first person says something defensive, look past it.*** Rather than responding negatively, stick with the issue or reassure your spouse about your connection.

4. Speak to the 49%: Most of our opinions are not 100% what we believe. Part of us sees a different viewpoint. Many opinions are 51% to 49%. So, when someone disagrees with you, instead of assuming they are entirely wrong, consider what part of them is speaking to your 49% and what part of you is speaking to their 49%. When trying to persuade someone, don't fight their 51%; appeal to their 49%. ***Awareness of the 51/49 breakdown helps foster unity even when we disagree.***

5. Increase positive communication: While it is good to reduce the amount of negative communication, some of it can't be avoided. There will always be misunderstandings, disagreements, and the need to communicate displeasure. While we can't eliminate all negative communication, there is no limit to how much positive communication we can use. ***Intentionally increase positive communication, and it will lessen the impact of negative communication.***

CONFLICT

Conflict is a natural part of any relationship, especially marriage. While some unnecessary conflict can be avoided by learning important skills and communicating correctly, the highest goal for a couple is not to become good at avoiding conflict but to become experts in handling conflict well. A healthy couple can experience the same conflict that threatens an unhealthy couple's connection and navigate it in such a way that it strengthens their connection and appreciation for each other.

Three Types of Fights

In her classic work *Hold Me Tight,* marriage expert Sue Johnson identifies three types of fights a married couple experiences. Being aware of these three types of conflicts is a useful way to process frustration positively. Johnson calls them the Demon Dialogues.

Find the Bad Guy

- **Blame.** Rather than focusing on the issue, the center of the debate revolves around which spouse is wrong.

- **Defensiveness.** Each will feel the need to defend themselves rather than recognize their role in the disagreement.

- **Rehashing.** The only conversation revolves around who said what, who did what, and disagreement over "facts."

- **Escalation.** A small issue becomes a major issue when the conflict becomes about the character of each spouse rather than the actual issue. Couples can even forget what the original disagreement was about.

- **Resolution.** The issue can never really be resolved because the issue has become about the spouses rather than the issue.

The Protest Polka

- **Dance.** A couple engages in a rhythm of behavior in which they don't see how their actions are responding and causing their partner's actions.

- **Pursue.** One spouse needs attention, so they pursue the attention of their spouse.

- **Withdraw.** The other spouse feels threatened, so they withdraw from their spouse.

- **Panic.** The withdrawal causes the pursuer to panic and to pursue harder, which creates panic and causes the one withdrawing to do so even more.

- **Reinforcement.** Both partners reinforce the fear of the other partner through their actions.

- **Pseudo-resolution.** Eventually, the connection is made, leading to a resolution. However, even the resolution reinforces the pattern. The one who withdraws feels the connection solves everything, and they think they won't have to connect like that again. The one who pursues will feel like the couple has made a breakthrough, and the level of connection will become the new norm. And so, they are set up for their next conflict.

Freeze and Flee

- **Emotional shutdown.** To protect their hearts, each partner shuts down emotionally, disconnecting from the marriage.

- **Avoidance.** Since conflict is never resolved and only leads to more pain, spouses stop bringing up issues and create an appearance of pseudo-peace.

- **Resignation.** Husband and wife resign themselves to the state of their marriage, believing there is nothing they can do to change the relationship.

- **Loneliness.** The result of freeze and flee is that both partners feel lonely and do not see each other as a possible fulfillment of that loneliness.

- **Notice:** Freezing and fleeing are the most dangerous state for a marriage. While it has less conflict and anger, it also lacks any sense of emotional connection.

Couples should learn to identify each of the Demon Dialogues and create ways to vocalize the pattern, step out of the fight, reframe the discussion, and productively find a resolution. Remember:

- Use hard words, but not harsh words.

- You're on the same team: it's us versus the issue, not me versus you.

- Critique actions, but don't criticize people.

- Don't be afraid to take a timeout, step out, cool down, and step back in (but make sure you always step back in; don't use a timeout to avoid conflict).

- Gottman reminds us that 70% of all conflicts can't be solved. It's not an issue of right versus wrong but a byproduct of different perspectives (due to things like personalities, family of origin, and past experience). While many conflicts can't be solved, they can effectively be managed.

THINK ABOUT IT BY YOURSELF

When you use non-secure communication, which form are you most likely to use? Why? Who in your life has modeled that form for you?

Consider each of the patterns of communication. Think about a person in your life who models one of those traits.

Who is someone that you communicate well with? Why? What allows that good communication to happen?

What is your pattern of handling conflict? When you get defensive, what causes the defensiveness?

What's your greatest weakness when it comes to conflict?

TALK ABOUT IT WITH YOUR SPOUSE

Discuss each of your family of origins regarding how communication and conflict were experienced. What form of communication did your parents use with you? What did they use with each other? How did your family of origin handle conflict?

Consider a time with your spouse in which conflict was handled well. What was the issue? How was it dealt with? Why did it go so well?

Consider a time with your spouse in which conflict was not handled well. What went wrong? Describe your personal actions which led to the conflict not going well.

Can you identify a time in which you have experienced each of the Demon Dialogues? Describe the experience.

If 70% of all conflict can't be resolved, what's an issue you have fought about that, in retrospect, wasn't an issue of right vs. wrong but was simply an issue of differing perspectives?

What's the circumstance in which you feel most comfortable communicating? How can you recreate those circumstances more often?

———————

"Healthy partners fight about issues.
Unhealthy partners fight about each other."
Pg. 128 FPL.

———————

DISCUSS IT AS A GROUP

How have communication styles in your family of origin affected how you communicate with your spouse? Discuss both positive and negative communication styles you bring to your relationship with your spouse.

If you could improve communication in your marriage, what's one thing you would do?

Of the three types of fights listed in this chapter, which one are you most likely to engage in? Which of the characteristics do you typically demonstrate?

What strategies do you use to minimize the negative and unconstructive conflict and communication in your marriage?

Identify one unsolvable conflict in your relationship that you have learned to manage. Describe how you have learned to manage this conflict and how your relationship has grown because of it.

Trust and respect are at the heart of good communication and conflict resolution. If I trust how you will treat my heart and respect the contributions you make to the relationship, we will learn to communicate well.

PRACTICE IT - BE INTENTIONAL

Calendar a specific time this week to communicate with each other. Take a walk or do an activity that allows for meaningful discussion.

Pick an issue and have a conversation about it while only using one of the non-secure forms of communication. How does it make you feel? How do non-secure communication styles make finding a resolution more difficult?

Pick a code word that each of you can use the next time you are in conflict and you recognize one of the Demon Dialogues. When the code word is used, stop the fight, step out, and discuss how you devolved into the Demon Dialogue.

DIGGING DEEPER

Friends, Partners, and Lovers by Kevin A. Thompson. Chapter 3, "No Wonder You Don't Love Each Other," and Chapter 4, "The Most Overlooked Characteristic of Marriage."

Hold Me Tight by Sue Johnson. Chapter 3, Conversation 1.

Crucial Conversations by Kerry Patterson et al.

SESSION 9

OTHERS

*"I love my children, but they are not equal partners in the family.
They are equal participants, but not equal partners." (pg.101, FPL)*

When husbands and wives say, "I do," they distinguish themselves from others and begin to create a unique sense of "us." At the same time, how they interact with others will significantly affect their bond.

The goal is to leverage their love for each other to benefit those around them and to allow others to positively influence their marriage. Problems occur when they allow outsiders to negatively impact the marriage—creating doubt, temptation, animosity, and weakening their commitment to each other.

Others are defined as anyone outside of the marital relationship—friends, co-workers, neighbors, strangers, in-laws, extended family, and children. These people must now be viewed differently than when the couple operated as individuals. ***Every relationship is changed*** when a husband and wife commit to one another.

If wives and husbands ***recognize the change, plan new patterns of behavior,*** and ***wisely choose how to interact with others,*** their marriage will be strengthened, they will avoid situations with dangerous consequences, and they will ***add to the well-being of others.***

BOUNDARIES WITH OTHERS

The difference between *us* and **them** is defined by a boundary. In the same way, a fence distinguishes my yard from my neighbor's yard, a boundary between people helps us understand what is appropriate and inappropriate. Marriage requires a series of boundaries to protect it.

Physical Boundaries:

- *All sexual contact is saved solely for one's spouse.* Nothing that could be construed as sexual contact can take place with another.
- *No forms of abuse are ever appropriate.* No, grabbing, pushing, hitting, or threatening to do so is ever acceptable.
- Except for an occasional surprise (buying a gift), *we never physically go places that we cannot tell our spouse.*
- *We respect each other's bodies and each individual's right to control their body.* Each spouse defines how and when they are touched, when they need personal space, and what levels of modesty they desire.

Emotional Boundaries:

- We share our emotional selves *first with our spouse* before sharing with others.
- We *nourish healthy same-sex friendships* for the purpose of accountability and support.
- *We do not share marital struggles with friends of the opposite sex.*
- Each spouse takes ownership of their emotions.

Time Boundaries:

- *We intentionally plan and guard time together with our spouse.*
- We create time for each spouse to *be alone and with friends.*
- As best as possible, *we limit work to work hours.*

Technological Boundaries:

- We *share passwords* and *do not have secret accounts.*
- We *limit time* spent on *social media, gaming,* and *other forms of technology.*
- We *set limits* and *create spaces* where phones are not used.

MORE ABOUT OTHERS

Friendships

We are relational beings. While marriage is the primary connection in our lives, **no individual was ever designed to fulfill all our relational needs.** We need other friends, relationships, and communities. A healthy marriage leverages others for their nourishment and growth, both individually and as a couple.

Individual Friends

- We each will **nourish individual friendships.**
- Our spouse doesn't have to interact with our friends, but **all friends must support our marriage and nourish our lives.**
- If friends hinder our growth or hurt our integrity, **we will intentionally give them up.**
- Friends are important but **should not be prioritized over our spouse or family.**

Couple Friends

- We will **nourish friendships with other couples.**
- We **prioritize having fun together** and with other people.
- We **intentionally** spend time with others who **value marriage, love us,** and **contribute to our lives.**

Communities

- *Couples grow in healthy communities.*
- We seek groups of people who v**alue marriage, family, and living God-honoring lives.**

We purposefully **build relationships** and **pour into the lives of others** with our **time, resources, and emotional energy.**

Parenting

The ultimate form of **others** is children. While our children are clearly an essential part of our family, they still must exist outside of our marriage.

- *We must distinguish our marriage relationship separate from our children.*
- If we prioritize our kids over our spouse, **both lose.**
- When we prioritize our spouse over our kids, **both win.**
  (Note: This distinction is not as clear in a blended family.)
- One of the best things you can do as a parent is to **love your spouse.**

Parenting is the perfect example of how we should *leverage the strength of our common bond for the well-being of others.* Few things are better for a child than a healthy marriage between their mom and dad. Yet parenting does create temptation to allow others to get between you and your spouse. Thankfully, marriage and parenting don't have to be at odds. *The key is to parent together from the foundation of a strong marriage.* Consider what a healthy marriage provides a child:

1. Creates a *secure environment.*

2. Models a *good relationship.*

3. Leads to *more affection between parents* which leads to *more affection with kids.*

4. *Reduces stress f*or both parents and children.

5. *Removes pressure* from kids to be the primary source of joy for their parents.

6. Gives a *sense of community.*

7. *Empowers the child to leave the family unit* without guilt as they grow.

Family
When a couple commits to each other, it is the *creation of a new family while two previous families remain.* How the three families interact is vital for a successful marriage.

- *Ignore* the two original families, and it *creates a void in our lives.*
- Continue to interact as though nothing has changed, and *our marriages will suffer.*
- Our marriage r*equires new patterns of connection* with our families.
- As a couple, we are *separate from our original families* while *still being active in those families.*

Separation means you, as a couple, *must make your own lives.* Parents become more friends than authority figures and providers. You and your spouse must distinguish yourselves from your families of origin and *form new traditions, patterns, and lives.* Parents (and other family members) must refrain from giving opinions without being asked.

Togetherness means that you will not only *continue to play a role in your family* of origin but will also *add to your family by bringing your spouse into the family.* We value our spouse's history, honor their family, and love them by loving those they love.
The two dangers we want to avoid are *enmeshment* and *disengagement.*

Enmeshment

- *To be enmeshed is to lack boundaries.*
- We can no longer distinguish between *us* (me and my spouse) and *them* (families, in-laws, and extended families).
- *Opinions* are given when they shouldn't be, and *family drama* defines most engagements.
- Enmeshed families often *can't understand when someone refuses to lose their own identity* into the larger identity of the family.

Disengagement

- The *opposite* of *enmeshment* is *disengagement.*
- We should *strive for healthy ways to stay involved in one another's lives* and *lovingly support each other even as we live our own lives.*
- Disengagement can lead to *estrangement, withholding emotional attachment,* and *intentionally hurting family members.*

Family Health

- We *make our own decisions, create our own identity,* and *bring strong attributes* to the larger family.
- We happily *serve others without being defined by them.*
- We express *empathy, compassion,* and *help* for the family without allowing their experiences to define ours.
- We find a *healthy balance* between being together and apart.
- We *help one another* without attempting to control the lives of others.
- Each spouse *takes responsibility* to communicate difficult news to their family of origin.

Holidays

An easy place to see how well families are *navigating the dynamic of being one family and three* is in the *celebration of holidays and big events* (birthdays, anniversaries, etc.). These types of family-focused days have the *potential to cause friction and negative emotions* in a marriage.

In a healthy relationship, a new marriage *recognizes the value and necessity of changing holiday traditions.* The following are suggestions to navigate setting new holiday traditions as a couple positively.

- Clearly discuss family traditions and negotiate how you as a couple want to spend the holidays and big family events.
- Discuss *family traditions* you want to *keep,* those you want to *change,* and new ones to *add.*
- Work together to compromise and to *create meaningful new traditions.*

- *Gracefully* and *lovingly communicate* to both families what you can and cannot do.
- Do your best to *share the holidays with family* while also *creating your own traditions.*
- While it's okay to mourn losing some family traditions, *it is not okay to manipulate or guilt your spouse or other family members* into your plans.

THINK ABOUT IT BY YOURSELF

What limits will you set regarding phones and other technology in the bedroom?

Looking at your family of origin, were they closer to being *enmeshed* or *disengaged?* What are some healthy traits they had that you want to emulate?

How do you create a strong sense of *us* so that no *other* can negatively impact your marriage?

For you, when does cheating become cheating?

What is one holiday tradition you loved that had to change when you got married?

List your closest friends as an individual and a couple. With a yes/no, identify if each friendship makes you a better person in a way that strengthens your marriage.

TALK ABOUT IT WITH YOUR SPOUSE

List several boundaries you will keep as a couple in each of the following areas: physical, emotional, time, and technology.

As a couple, who are your closest friends? Do you regularly prioritize time spent together with those couples? Identify one couple you would like to get to know better.

What are some strengths that you as a couple possess that can be leveraged for the well-being of others?

What is something you would like to learn as a couple? Who is a couple who possess that ability or character trait that can teach you?

How do you love your children without letting them negatively impact your marriage?

Identify who are the others who bring your relationship the most danger and who are the others who can most benefit your connection.

While marriage is the primary connection in our lives, *no individual was ever designed to fulfill all our relational needs.* We need other friends, relationships, and communities.

DISCUSS IT AS A GROUP

Are you in greater threat of enmeshment or disengagement from each of your families? Why?

Discuss where lack of boundaries has destroyed relationships.

What is one boundary you and your spouse disagree on? How can you find a workable solution?

Discuss how your friends (both individual and couple) have enhanced your life. Have you had friends who have had a negative influence on your life and/or relationship with your spouse?

How can you create or be a part of a healthy community that helps your marriage?

Are you happy with how you currently celebrate the holidays? Is there anything you would change? Do you see any change ahead based on a change in life stage?

Does parenting draw you closer together as a couple or pull you apart? Why?

PRACTICE IT - BE INTENTIONAL

Take an afternoon and create a set of family values. Define what is most important to you and what will define your relationship. (See the Family Values Scripter)

Pick a night to not use technology. Have dinner, go for a walk, spend time together, and go to bed without checking your phone or watching something on a device.

Schedule a date night with two new couples to establish a new connection.

DIGGING DEEPER

Stay In Your Lane by Kevin A. Thompson.

SESSION 10

PRIORITIZE SEX

*"When both spouses make the pleasure of the other their highest goal,
sex reaches a new level of intimacy and meaning." (pg. 179, FPL)*

(Note: this chapter focuses on a very sensitive topic. It is written with a generally healthy marriage in mind. If there is any addiction, abuse, or adultery involved, seek the advice of a professional counselor.)

Sex is often viewed mistakenly in one of two ways:

1. Some believe it is a secondary issue (at times even considered sinful). They think sex shouldn't greatly matter if a couple is genuinely in love.

2. Others view it as the primary issue, believing sex is the most important thing.

Neither viewpoint is correct. Sex is neither secondary nor ultimate. **Instead, it is one of the three major aspects of a healthy marriage.** If we elevate it to being the ultimate thing, we are assuring disaster. If we devalue it, we are courting disconnection. A wise couple will prioritize it properly.

In his work *Eight Dates*, John Gottman simplifies good sex down to two basic ideas: **friendship** and **priority.** When a couple builds a strong friendship with each other and chooses to prioritize sexual intimacy, they usually have a strong connection as lovers. Eliminate either of those, and the sexual connection will likely struggle (Gottman et al., 2019).

Of course, I would add the importance of **partnership** as well. When one person isn't pulling their weight in the productivity of the household, it erodes the erotic connection between spouses. Especially for couples raising kids, the physical and emotional toll demands the full involvement of both husband and wife. To check out of a partnership but expect intimacy is foolish.

When a couple creates a strong friendship and partnership, it gives them all the tools necessary to build a meaningful life of intimacy.

MORE ABOUT PRIORITIZING SEX IN YOUR MARRIAGE

The key word regarding intimacy is the word mutual. Too often, intimacy can become primarily about the pleasure of one spouse to the hindrance of the other. When this happens, the potential for meaningful intimacy is lost. The pathway for good sex is a *mutual pursuit* of *mutual pleasure* for the purpose of *mutual connection.*

Mutual Pursuit

- Both spouses must *prioritize* the creation of a meaningful sex life.
- It's a *pursuit,* not a destination. It's an ongoing journey together through each season of life.
- The pursuit consists of *individual work* (each exploring what might keep them from giving themselves to the other) and *couple work* (together doing the work and getting the help necessary to accomplish the goal.)
- Focus on heading in the right direction, not necessarily expecting continual improvement. We succeed, fail, learn, and grow. *Some seasons won't be very good, but we keep going.*
- The pursuit itself adds to our *friendship* and *partnership.*

Mutual Pleasure

- Any single experience can be geared toward one partner, but the *holistic approach of intimacy must be about both partners.*
- *Individually,* we must understand what we like/dislike to communicate it with our partner.
- *Together,* we should seek how to give and receive pleasure to one another.
- Sex that's good for him may not be good for her. *Sex that's good for her is almost always good for him.*

Mutual Connection

- *Sex is ultimately about connection.* We want to feel seen, valued, and loved. Sex is one way that happens.
- John Gottman says that up to 25% of attempts at sex won't happen (headache, kids walk in, the day doesn't go as planned). *While the attempt might fail, a connection can still occur.*

- Sex is one of the few acts that, ideally, ***puts a couple's full attention on each other,*** communicating that each is uniquely special to the other.

- It is ***connection,*** not physical prowess, that makes for truly great sex.

We Must Learn to Talk About It

If mutual connection and pleasure are the result of mutual pursuit, a key to that pursuit is ***conversation.*** In our Friends, Partners & Lovers assessment, 77% of respondents show hesitation in talking to their spouse about their sex lives. With open and honest communication, a couple has a chance to create a life of intimacy that is meaningful for both partners.

Here are some tips for those who struggle to discuss sex :

How To Talk About It

- ***Speak carefully and softly.*** Recognize it's a very personal topic that can cause harm when spoken about incorrectly.

- ***Don't talk about it in bed.*** Take a walk, go for a drive, or find someplace quiet, but don't review the act right after it happened or talk about it where it's most likely to occur.

- ***Don't allow hurt feelings to stop the conversation.*** You are both learning how to communicate. If your partner says something hurtful, discuss it, forgive each other, and keep talking.

- ***When necessary, get help.*** A couple of sessions with a counselor can go a long way with this topic. Don't be afraid to get the help you need if you struggle to talk about it with each other. (This includes getting a **physical exam** and having frank discussions with your doctor about what is happening physically with your body.)

What to Talk About

- ***Insecurities and fears.*** What makes you afraid? How can your partner make you feel safe?

- ***Differing viewpoints.*** Spouses often see sex in different ways. Don't expect your spouse to see it or value it the same way you do. Don't try to convince them of your way, but ***seek to understand their perspective.***

- ***Turn-offs and Turn-ons.*** What do you like? What do you dislike?

- ***Hygiene.*** Be honest with your partner if they need to shower before an encounter or brush their teeth before kissing.

- ***What worked?*** One of the best things to tell your spouse is what they do well.

Three Types of Sex

Not all sex is the same. Most couples will need to have at least *three different types of encounters* to have a healthy connection.

Spontaneous

A couple should never lose their sense of *spontaneity*. There should be moments in which the mood hits, and they enjoy each other's company. While this happens easily early in a marriage, they must *use intention to maintain this free experience* throughout their relationship. *Spontaneous sex will help a couple steer clear of a rut.*

Scheduled

As work and family demands increase, *scheduled sex* becomes more important. While some believe scheduling intimacy ruins the mood, nothing could be farther from the truth. Scheduling Christmas doesn't hurt Christmas; it sets expectations. *So, too, scheduling sex can create a sense of excitement and expectation.* The busier one's life with work and kids, the more sex needs to be scheduled so both partners can be fully engaged in the act.

Maintenance

Rarely is a couple in perfect *compatibility* with the desired frequency of sex. A way to navigate this is to occasionally have *maintenance sex,* which is geared more at one partner rather than the other. *Note: make sure that maintenance sex doesn't become the only type of intimacy a couple experiences.*

SOME FINAL THOUGHTS ABOUT PRIORITIZING SEX IN YOUR MARRIAGE

Sex is a powerful element of every marriage. *The question is whether it will be a powerful source of connection or a powerful source of conflict.* In many cases, sex is a barometer of the relationship. When all conditions are right, sex is good. When an area of life gets out of kilter, it often expresses itself in the bedroom.

Challenges

- *Rarely do problems originate in the bedroom, but they often show up there.*
- If sex is a point of contention, consider the strength of your *friendship* and *partnership* first before assuming the actual problem is sex. If you strengthen the first two, the latter often takes care of itself.

Stereotypes

- Be careful regarding stereotypes and Hollywood expectations regarding sex. ***We often do not properly understand what is and isn't normal in the bedroom.***
- The stereotype is that men want sex more than women. Yet, surveys show that in 30% of relationships, women desire more sex than men. If you are in such a relationship, it's easy to feel like something is wrong with you because you don't fit the cultural norm.

Assumptions

- ***People regularly assume that sex should be easy.*** Movies and social media rarely tell stories of good marriages where couples struggle with intimacy.
- ***Every couple will have seasons in which creating a meaningful sex life is a challenge.*** Expect times of difficulty, but keep on working to create the marriage you desire.

THINK ABOUT IT BY YOURSELF

Consider what early messages you learned about sex. Was it talked about? Was it seen as good, bad, or indifferent?

Shame has a negative impact on our sexual experience. What is your experience with shame, and how does it impact you?

If you could help your spouse understand one thing about sex from your perspective, what would it be?

Is there anything from your past that could (or should) cause your spouse to be hesitant with you regarding intimacy?

What or who has had the greatest impact on you regarding what you think about sex? Is there anything you need to relearn in order to have a proper perspective?

———————

"Sex in real life is so complex and personal that we often trade meaningful sex for a marriage."
Pg. 156, FPL

———————

TALK ABOUT IT WITH YOUR SPOUSE

When you think about sex with your spouse, what are your three favorite memories?

Describe a time in which sex didn't go as planned, yet you both handled it well, and it drew you closer together. What made it go right?

Consider a time in which sex was planned, and it didn't go well. Tell your spouse of a way you could have handled things differently.

What are some things you have not had an open conversation with each other about? How can you create a space of safety to have those honest conversations?

If you disagree on frequency, each of you states how many times a week (or month) you would prefer. How far apart are you? What would it take to close the gap? Is the issue really frequency, or is something else at play?

Of the three areas, mutual pursuit, pleasure, and connection, which do you think the two of you do the best at, and which area do you think you could best improve?

How have weaknesses in your friendship or partnership negatively impacted your sex life? How can you improve those areas?

DISCUSS IT AS A GROUP

How do you feel discussing issues like sex and intimacy with another couple? Are you nervous?

How does sex change through the different seasons of life?
What are the lessons learned through each season?

How have you overcome challenges in your sex life through the years? How do we use difficulty to drive us together rather than tearing us apart?

What is the best way to communicate needs and desires, especially as they change over time?

How do we maintain strong sexual boundaries in our lives while also learning and growing regarding intimacy?

If a couple has a healthy sex life, what does that mean?

PRACTICE IT - BE INTENTIONAL

Schedule a specific time this week to discuss your sex lives. Plan a place where you can go for a walk, hike, or ride and have a meaningful conversation about what you are getting right, things you might like to improve and plan your next time of connection.

If you are in a generally healthy spot, plan a weekend getaway meant to focus on rejuvenating your intimacy. Do other things besides sex, but make sex the primary focus of the getaway.

If you are in a rut, intentionally set a time when you will change things up. Change times, places in the house, and/or position to give some variety.

DIGGING DEEPER

Friends, Partners, and Lovers by Kevin A. Thompson. Chapters 11-14.

Gottman, J., et al. (2019). *Eight Dates: Essential Conversations for a Lifetime of Love.* Workman Publishing Company.

The Invisible Bond: How to Break Free from Your Sexual Past by Barbara Wilso

Kiss Me Again: Restoring Lost Intimacy in Marriage by Barbara Wilson

SESSION 11

INTIMACY AND VULNERABILITY

"To become lifetime lovers, be willing to keep trying, failing, and trying again." (pg. 175, FPL)

Lovers create a meaningful sex life, but being lovers is about more than just sex. Intimacy happens outside of sex, and sex can be devoid of intimacy. ***Healthy couples nourish a meaningful life of intimacy, which includes but is not limited to sexual activity.***

If ***friendship*** is symbolized by walking side-by-side through life and ***partnership*** is about having each other's back, then ***lovers*** are about facing one another, seeing each other fully, and loving one another completely.

This face-to-face interaction requires ***vulnerability***. In marriage, we are emotionally and physically exposed in ways unlike any other relationship in life. In part, this is a beautiful invitation to marriage. In a culture where we are often unseen, abused, and exploited, ***marriage offers a safe and secure relationship with someone who will see you and love you completely.***

Yet, this is also a threat to marriage. When we do not love each other well, we will reinforce the negative messages of the world: messages like something is wrong with you, you don't deserve to be loved, and no one can be trusted.

Marriage allows you to create a relationship in which you can ***safely reveal the deepest (and sometimes darkest) aspects of your soul,*** knowing you will be accepted, loved, and treated with kindness. Yet because of past hurts, there is a constant temptation to hide the parts of yourself that you fear are unlovable.

Thus, the difficulty regarding vulnerability. *We can't experience true intimacy without vulnerability.* But life has taught us that to avoid pain, we should never be vulnerable. *This is a challenge of marriage—to create a relationship where we grow in vulnerability, nourish intimacy, and continually experience a greater and deeper love through every season.*

TRUST + RESPECT = VULNERABILITY

While it's not a clear-cut formula, there is a need to create reasonable levels of trust and respect before we attempt vulnerability. Many relationships are sabotaged early in dating because one partner gets vulnerable before the other person has proven themselves trustworthy. We must show that we will treat each other's hearts right and be wise in what we say and do before expecting transparency in intimate parts of our lives. *But as trust and respect grow, so can vulnerability.* Here are five areas in which we should pursue intimacy.

Emotional

- Sharing one's true thoughts and feelings.
- Recognizing the value and legitimacy of emotions and supporting each other without judgment.
- Giving emotional support to one another
- Grieving the losses of life together.
- Celebrating success and encouraging one another.
- Checking in with each other to see how one's heart is.
- Being a source of stability and strength for each other.

Physical

- Hugging, kissing, holding hands
- Cuddling
- Extended eye contact
- Massage
- Leveraging each other's bodies to lower blood pressure, increase oxytocin, etc.

Mental

- Brainstorming ideas
- Learning from each other's different life experiences
- Engaging in deep conversations
- Solving problems together
- Encouraging each other's personal growth

Spiritual

- Praying for and with one another
- Worshipping together
- Serving with each other

Experiential

- Telling our story to one another
- Revealing hurts, griefs, and sorrows
- Sharing experiences together and holding those memories across the years
- Traveling

The Power of Touch

Non-sexual touch is extremely powerful, and it is a vital part of a healthy marriage. We know this as relationships begin. A dating couple often looks for every excuse to touch—to hold hands, brush arms, or put a hand on the other's shoulder.

Touch is so powerful that an inappropriate relationship crosses a major line the first time a touch occurs. When feelings are expressed in touch, there is often no turning back from the relationship.

But touch can also be used in a positive way. It can:

- ***Ease the tension*** in a tough conversation.
- ***Communicate support*** when words are hard to find.
- ***Quietly comfort*** when silence is necessary.

Touch is a powerful weapon in the arsenal of marriage. Yet, too often, we fail to use it. There is a direct correlation between marital satisfaction and the amount of non-sexual touch. If you want to improve your marriage, touch more often. ***Do the following and see what happens.***

- Every time you pass one another, *touch.*
- Anytime you leave the house, *kiss.*
- When you return home from the day, *hug for at least 10 seconds.*
- When you are walking, *hold hands.*
- When seated next to each other, *put a hand on the other's leg.*
- When watching TV, *sit together and cuddle.*
- When going to bed, *hold one another until at least one of you goes to sleep.*

Lack of Non-Sexual Touching

There are two primary reasons why a married couple may not be touching:

1. **Apathy.** Through a *lack of intention,* a couple can slowly stop touching. If this is the case, the above list is all the couple needs. *With just a little intention,* a couple can reignite their non-sexual touch and, in so doing, can dramatically improve their relationship.

2. **An Absence of Trust and/or Respect.** When trust wanes, so does touch. *We do not have trouble touching our spouse unless we no longer respect them and feel safe around them.* If the above list is difficult, something is wrong. Trying harder will not " help. You need to seek professional help to understand why non-sexual touch is difficult between you.

Few things can change your relationship as dramatically and quickly as non-sexual touch. *Be intentional, have fun, and see how a little touch can go a long way.*

Vulnerability

Being vulnerable is an important part of life. It can help us with family, friendships, and work and can be a key component of being healthy as an individual. *But vulnerability doesn't come naturally.* A healthy marriage can be the greatest classroom in which we learn how and when to be vulnerable. We can then take that skill to every other aspect of life.
Here are some ways to learn vulnerability:

- If you struggle with vulnerability or if it doesn't come naturally, *admit it*. Ask for help in being vulnerable.

- *Spend time around young children and learn from them.* Before they grow up, kids tend to be very vulnerable.

- *Learn to recognize and communicate feelings.* Many, especially men, do not have the language to communicate what they are feeling. We must learn the language of vulnerability. (Consider an emotion wheel that gives a variety of words for different feelings.)

- *Admit mistakes.* Few things connect us with others as much as admitting when we have done something wrong and communicating regret about that action.

- *Share uncertainties and fears.* You don't have to have it all together; tell your spouse when you are unsure about what to do.

- Learn the difference between *genuine vulnerability* and *relational manipulation* through pseudo-vulnerability. Some, especially those with anxious attachment, can play the role of victim to protect themselves. It looks like vulnerability but isn't. Know the difference.

- *Ask questions* that go below the surface and *be genuinely concerned* for others, especially your spouse.

MORE ABOUT INTIMACY

7 Red Flags for Dying Intimacy

If you aren't growing, you are dying. It's true for every aspect of a relationship, including intimacy. Before death occurs, there are warning signs. Wise couples watch for these red flags and take swift action when they see a warning.

1. **A decline in non-sexual touch.** When it comes to intimacy, our first thoughts go to the bedroom, but the first danger signs occur outside the bedroom. *Non-sexual touch is a wonderful sign of intimacy between spouses.* Hand-holding, reaching out for one another rather than avoiding each other, and any instance of good touch bonds a couple together. *As spouses, oftentimes subconsciously, begin to pull away from each other, the first evidence is a decline in non-sexual touch.*

2. **Avoiding eye contact.** Few things are as intimate as eye contact. One of the first signs that someone is romantically interested in another is lingering eye contact. Whereas two people without romantic feelings might look one another in the eye and then look away, when interest is present, eyes linger longer. When eye contact is avoided, intimacy is declining. *Be intentional about looking your spouse in the eyes; it will draw you closer to them.*

3. **An absence of playfulness.** There is a direct correlation between intimacy and fun–just look at the interaction between a mother and newborn. As a mother bonds with her child, she plays games, laughs, and engages the child. Even the most mundane of tasks–

eating or changing a diaper–includes playfulness. *Healthy couples enjoy one another's company. They laugh, joke, seek out fun, and try to make difficult things more enjoyable.* As playfulness dwindles, so does intimacy.

4. **Sex becomes a task.** *Good sex is an intimate act that draws two people together.* It is a physical act, but it has a greater impact emotionally and spiritually. When sex no longer touches our soul, intimacy is dying. *Not every physical connection will touch us in a deep way, but when it doesn't ever draw us together, we are in trouble.* There are moments when sex is a chore, but if it's always a chore, something is wrong.

5. **Increase in individual thinking.** When intimacy is deep, a couple continually thinks from an "us" perspective. *Everything is about our dreams, our desires, our goals, and our future.* As intimacy declines, spouses begin to view things more individually. This change from "we" to "I" and from "us" to "me" is a sign of what is happening inside of us. Maybe we are growing apart from our spouse. Maybe we feel isolated because they aren't carrying their weight in the relationship. *It's natural to experience seasons of isolation, but when our thoughts are dominated by our individual selves instead of one another, we must reconnect with our spouse.*

6. **Conversation is all business.** A key component of marriage is partnership. My spouse isn't just my lover; she is also my partner in life. Because we are "in business" together, many of our conversations will be about work–who is taking the kids where, how are we going to pay the bills, what is happening with her job, and my job. *While we must talk about the business side of marriage on a daily basis, we must be intentional to make sure that isn't all we talk about.* When conversation loses all content about our hearts, dreams, and aspirations, intimacy is dying.

7. **Turning toward others rather than spouse.** When good or bad things happen, we want to tell others. We can't help it. We naturally run toward community when things happen in our lives. *In healthy couples, they turn toward one another first. Before a friend, co-worker, or confidant, spouses seek each other.* When a friend replaces a spouse as our "first person," our intimacy with our spouse is dying.

Intentionally Building Intimacy

These seven red flags that warn of dying intimacy *also point out opportunities for building intimacy.* If you want to build a closer bond with your spouse:

- *Intentionally* increase non-sexual touch
- Look one another in the *eye*
- *Be playful* with each other
- Attempt to make an *emotional connection* during sex

- *Think "we"* more than "me."
- *Talk about your heart* rather than your tasks
- *Make your spouse your first-person*

A little intention in each of these areas can go a long way toward increasing the feelings of intimacy. Dying intimacy doesn't have to lead to a dead relationship. It can be the catalyst for relational success if a couple recognizes it and does something about it.

THINK ABOUT IT BY YOURSELF

Who is the most vulnerable person you know that you also deeply respect? What allows them to be so vulnerable?

How did your family of origin treat vulnerability and intimacy? Did you feel completely safe with each parent? Were you able to communicate your true thoughts and feelings?

Apart from your spouse, who is the person with whom you feel most comfortable being vulnerable? What do they do that makes you trust them?

Outside of sex, what type of intimacy makes you feel the most valued and loved?

Consider a time in which you didn't act in a safe way for your spouse. If you could do it over again, what would you do?

Is there any way in which you have become apathetic in your relationship?

TALK ABOUT IT WITH YOUR SPOUSE

Describe one of your favorite (non-sexual) moments of intimacy with your spouse. What made it memorable? How could you experience more times like that?

Is there a small habit you could include in your daily rhythm that would increase your feeling of intimacy? (Hug every day, kiss before you leave, etc.)

On an average day, how many times a day do you touch each other? How can you double that number?

Of the five types of intimacy, which is your strength? Which contains your greatest chance for growth?

Describe how your parents showed affection for you as a child.
Did it change as you aged? Do you wish they would have done something different?

Choose one thing you can add to your intimacy to see how it might impact your relationship.

"We are foolish if we think we can hold strong affections for one another without any effort," pg. 172, FPL.

DISCUSS IT AS A GROUP

Why is physical touch a need for everyone, not just those who think it's their love language?

What are elements of intimacy outlined in this chapter that you never considered were a part of it?

Of the 7 Red Flags of Dying intimacy, which sticks out to you as something happening in your relationship?

How do we combat apathy in marriage, specifically when it comes to intimacy?

How does non-sexual intimacy impact sexual intimacy? Why does increasing non-sexual touch often have a positive impact on sexual touch?

What prevents you from being truly vulnerable with others?

PRACTICE IT - BE INTENTIONAL

Write a letter to your spouse that includes why you love each other and recount three of your favorite days you can remember with each other. Tell why those days were so important.

Take your spouse to your elementary playground. Tell them the story of what you remember as your most embarrassing moment in elementary school. What happened? What did you feel? If you could tell that child one thing, what would it be?

Have one partner sit on the couch while the other lays down with their head in your lap. Stroke their hair as they relax, and after twenty minutes, switch.

———

Vulnerability is rarely easy. By learning to talk with our mentors about our marriage, we can learn to talk with each other about issues that matter.

———

DIGGING DEEPER

Friends, Partners, and Lovers by Kevin A. Thompson. Chapters 11-14.

Gottman, J., et al. (2019). *Eight Dates: Essential Conversations for a Lifetime of Love.* Workman Publishing Company.

SESSION 12

F A I T H

"Be intentional." (pg. 205, FPL)

Faith is more than a personal belief. It's a perspective of life that impacts what we value, pursue, and do. For a couple, a meaningful faith creates a coherent operating system by which every element of family life is brought into compatibility.

For a life of faith to have a full impact on a marriage and family, it must be running in two realms—the ***individual*** and the ***community.*** Each person must experience a personal faith that impacts their lives, directs their decisions, and provides a perspective on life that is different than what comes naturally. Then, together, they must choose to allow God to direct their marriage so they are living by the teachings of Jesus in practice and not just in name only.

LET GOD GUIDE YOUR MARRIAGE

While there are many characteristics of a God-guided marriage, some are more important than others.

    Separately Seek God

- A God-guided marriage begins as ***each individual seeks a healthy relationship with God.***

- The faith of one partner isn't enough for both partners. Both should seek God and develop a vibrant spiritual life as individuals.

- No matter where your spouse is spiritually, ***you can deepen your own faith.***

Jointly Seek God

- Building on the foundation of two individuals having a relationship with God, *a couple can jointly seek Him.*

- This happens in a variety of ways but can include *worshipping together, serving together, and studying together.*

- By seeking God together, your relationship as a couple will be stronger, and your personal relationship with God will also reap benefits.

- *Live Out God's Commands with One Another.* All the *"one-another"* passages in the New Testament can be directly applied to a married couple.

- *"Love one another" "honor one another"* and *"submit to one another,"* can help you live out a God guided marriage. The Bible says very little directly about marriage, but the whole message of Scripture influences our understanding of marriage. *The New Testament commands can be used as guidelines within marital relationships.*

Allow God to Define Success and Failure

- We are greatly influenced by our culture. But what a successful marriage looks like to Western society is not what a successful relationship looks like to God.

- Western culture defines happiness as the main goal; *the Bible says Christ-likeness is a greater symbol of success.*

- Society might honor money, power, and influence. *Jesus would value love, sacrifice, and kindness.* while seeing money and influence as blessings from God and tools for furthering His kingdom.

- A God-guided marriage *recognizes* the temptation of culture, *rejects* its view of success, and *follows* God.

Continually Pursue One Another

- One advantage of a God-guided marriage should be a higher view of the marital relationship, which results in a stronger work ethic. When a marriage is directed by God, *both spouses work intentionally and diligently to make a strong and thriving marriage.*

- *Apathy in marriage is never God-ordained.* Instead, God's leadership results in a desire to do the work, be vulnerable, learn new skills, get help, forgive, move forward, and improve.

- In part, *marriage was designed for the purpose of transforming our hearts.* As we experience hardship, struggles, and misunderstandings, couples guided by God see these as opportunities to identify ways that we need to change.

- By doing the work necessary, we not only become more like God but also experience a growing intimacy with one another.

Learn From and Teach Others

- Apart from God, it's tempting to look at marriage as solely personal. However, a *Christian always views good things as opportunities to bless others.*

- *A God-guided marriage is one which is quick to assist others by passing on what they have learned.* Through support, encouragement, and frank conversations, we help others and hope they experience joy in their relationships.

- *We should also be quick to learn from others,* humbly recognizing that we always have room for improvement.

- A *wise couple always has older mentors* helping to show them the way while also *being quick to assist younger couples* seeking assistance with their relationships.

A God-guided marriage is different from other relationships. While outwardly, it may look like other marriages, the motivations of a couple seeking to please God greatly differ from those who do not seek God's glory. God's presence in a relationship may not diminish the amount of conflict a couple experiences, but it does greatly change how that couple handles conflict. *When we seek to follow God, we are more long-suffering, kind, thoughtful, compassionate, and grace-filled with our spouses.* While seeking God doesn't ensure a marriage that lasts, it does greatly improve the chances of success.

MORE ABOUT FAITH AND YOUR MARRIAGE

Serve

What is one step the average couple can take to improve their marriage? This is a question I often receive, and my answer is always the same. If a couple is reasonably healthy (no addiction, abuse, or adultery) and they generally love each other, one of the best steps they can take to improve their marriage is to serve together.

Serve Together

- Find opportunities to consistently serve alongside each other. That might be the two of you doing something together or simply serving at the same time and for the same cause.

- Try to find something that utilizes your unique blend of personality, temperament, and experience where the two of you can contribute together.

- Strive to get your marriage to a place where you can serve other couples by encouraging their pursuit of a healthy marriage.

Serve One Another

- Service outside of the home should lead to service inside the home.
- Allow a heart of service to invade everything you do as individuals and as a couple.
- Never confuse your spouse or children by serving outside the home more than you serve each other.

Community

Marriage is ultimately between two people, but it has a much larger impact than just those two people, and its success is dependent on more than just the husband and wife. We are meant to live in community, and an integral part of marital success is finding the right communities and allowing them to influence our connection with each other.

Peers Who Are With You

- We all need friends who walk alongside us through life.
- They aren't the experts; we aren't the experts. Together, we are trying to figure things out.
- We support each other as we walk through the seasons of life.
- Because of life's transitions, we are always in the process of making new friends and expanding our circle of influence.

Mentors Who Guide You

- Everyone benefits from having others who encourage and support us.
- Mentors come in various styles. Some are clearly defined; others are just lifelong friends who we can depend on throughout the journey.
- Mentors aren't counselors, but we can learn through their mistakes and/or successes.

Heroes Who Inspire You

- While mentors are close relationships, heroes are those we watch from afar.
- Heroes are people who inspire us to love each other more.

Friends Who Follow You

- We can serve others by encouraging them in their relationship.
- Others can benefit from our experiences.
- Serving others will also strengthen our relationship.

Divorce is often contagious. It's not unusual for whole friend groups to experience multiple divorces at the same time. In the same way, healthy marriages tend to give birth to other healthy marriages. Few things can help our connection, like putting ourselves in communities of couples who value marriage, work on their relationship, and encourage others in the same pursuit.

_____

Show me a marriage with a high gratitude quotient and I'll show you a happy marriage.

_____

Gratitude

Marriage has seasons of great difficulty. And some marriages are harder than others. But marriage was never meant to be the hardest thing you do. Instead, it's meant to be a source of encouragement and support as you navigate the challenges of life.

That's the potential for every couple. We can create such a strong connection that whatever is going on in us, between us, or beyond us, we feel a deep sense of gratitude for the life that God has given to us and the relationship we have with each other.

_____

When we fail to see how fleeting this season of life is, we miss the joy and goodness of the moment.

_____

Marriage isn't forever. It is a temporary gift God gives us on earth, not to be duplicated in heaven. While it has its challenges, an integral aspect of a healthy relationship is having a deep sense of gratitude for one another.

As we work on ourselves and our relationship, gratitude begins to grow within us. Wherever you are in your marriage, you are here, you are together, and God has given you another day to love each other well. Thank Him for that opportunity. And from a sense of gratitude, approach this season of your life and your marriage.

THINK ABOUT IT BY YOURSELF

What has your history of faith looked like? Did you grow up in the church? What is your personal belief about God?

In the past, what has been your favorite way to serve others? What do you get out of service?

If you had to narrow down your life of faith to one verse of Scripture, what would it be?

Who are couples that have marriages you look to as a model?

TALK ABOUT IT WITH YOUR SPOUSE

Who do you want to be as a couple in regard to faith?

What does it mean to you for God to guide your marriage?

What are two ways that you can serve together?

Who is a couple that you would like to get to know more about in hopes that they can be a strong example of a good marriage to you?

Identify at least one younger couple that you would like to invest in their marriage. (Note: you may not be ready yet to make a difference for someone else, but make it a goal to get healthy enough that God can use you in the life of someone else.)

DISCUSS IT AS A GROUP

Who are the people of faith that you most admire? What is it about them that creates admiration?

What does it look like to seek God separately and to seek Him together?

What are some ways to grow in our faith?

What causes you to be a mentor couple? How does the process help your connection with each other?

How has God guided your marriage? Are there examples of when you didn't follow His way and now regret it?

How do we remain grateful for each other while at the same time discussing issues that need to be changed?

PRACTICE IT - BE INTENTIONAL

Attend a church service together that's of a different denominational perspective than what you are used to. Notice what they get right. What was new to you?

Take a walk this week or plan a date night and have a meaningful conversation about who you want to be as a couple. What are the character traits you want to build?

Pick a book of the Bible or a devotional book. For one week, each read a section and then have a time later when you discuss.

DIGGING DEEPER

Happily by Kevin A. Thompson.

BIBLIOGRAPHY

Chapman, Gary. The Five Love Languages: How to Express Heartfelt Commitment to Your Mate (Northfield, 1992)

Clark, Mark. The Problem of God (Zondervan, 2017)
        The Problem of Jesus (Zondervan, 2021)

Cron, I.M. & Stabile, S. The Road Back to You (Intervarsity, 2016)

Gregoire, Shelia Wray. The Great Sex Rescue (Baker, 2021)

Gottman, John. The Seven Principles for Making Marriage Work (Random House, 1999)
        Eight Dates: Essential Conversations for a Lifetime of Love (Workman, 2019)

Housel, Morgan. The Psychology of Money (Harriman House, 2020)

Johnson, Sue. Hold Me Tight (Little Brown Spark, 2008)

Keller, Timothy. Every Good Endeavor (Penguin Books, 2014)

Patterson, Kerry et al. Crucial Conversations (McGraw, 2012)

Ramsey, Dave. The Total Money Makeover (Thomas Nelson, 2013)

Thompson, Kevin A. Friends, Partners & Lovers: What It Takes to Make Marriage Work (Revell, 2017)
        Fearless Families: Building Brave Homes in an Uncertain World (Cook, 2021)
        Happily: 8 Commitments of Couples who Laugh, Love, and Last (Revell, 2018)
        Stay In Your Lane: How to worry less, love more, and get things done. (Thrive, 2023)

Wilson, Barbara. The Invisible Bond: How to Break Free from Your Sexual Past (Multnomah, 2006)
        Kiss Me Again: Restoring Lost Intimacy in Marriage. (Multnomah, 2020)

THE AUTHORS

Kevin A. Thompson is a husband, father, and Married Life Pastor at Bayside Church in the Greater Sacramento Region. The author of multiple books, including, Friends, Partners & Lovers, Fearless Families, and Stay In Your Lane, Kevin is passionate about seeing families thrive. Originally from Arkansas, Kevin has been a frequent guest on Focus on the Family, Family Life, and featured in the New York Times. He writes at changetheodds.com. He and his wife, Jenny, along with their two children reside in Auburn, CA.

Dr. Randy Nordell has been married to Kelly for 35 years, and they have been involved in small groups and working with and mentoring young couples for most of their married life. They have two adult children who are both married. Professionally, Randy has been an educator for 35 years and a college textbook author for the past 15 years. When not teaching and writing, he enjoys spending time with his family and friends, cycling, skiing, backpacking, reading, cooking, and traveling.